THE TANTRIC DISTINCTION

OTHER WORKS BY JEFFREY HOPKINS

The Buddhism of Tibet and the Key to the Middle Way

Buddhist Advice for Living and Liberation: Nāgārjuna's Precious Garland

Calm Abiding and Special Insight

Compassion in Tibetan Buddhism

Cutting Through Appearances:
The Practice and Theory of Tibetan Buddhism

The Dalai Lama at Harvard

Death, Intermediate State, and Rebirth in Tibetan Buddhism

Deity Yoga

Emptiness in the Mind-Only School of Buddhism

Emptiness Yoga

Fluent Tibetan: A Proficiency Oriented Learning System,
Novice and Intermediate Levels

Health Through Balance: An Introduction to Tibetan Medicine

The Kālachakra Tantra: Rite of Initiation for the Stage of Generation

Kindness, Clarity, and Insight

The Meaning of Life From a Buddhist Perspective

Meditation on Emptiness

Meditative States in Tibetan Buddhism

Sex, Orgasm, and the Mind of Clear Light: The Sixty-Four Arts of Gay
Male Love

Tantra in Tibet

Tantric Practice in Nyingma

Tibetan Arts of Love

THE TANTRIC DISTINCTION

A Buddhist's Reflections on Compassion and Emptiness

Jeffrey Hopkins

Edited by Anne C. Klein

Revised edition

Wisdom Publications • Boston

Wisdom Publications
199 Elm Street
Somerville MA 02144 USA

First published in 1984
Revised edition, 1999

Library of Congress Cataloging-in-Publication Data
Hopkins, Jeffrey.
    The tantric distinction : a Buddhist's reflections on compassion
and emptiness / Jeffrey Hopkins ; edited by Anne C. Klein.—Rev. ed.
        p.   cm.
    Includes bibliographical references and index.
    ISBN 0-86171-154-8 (paper : alk. paper)
        1. Tantric Buddhism—Doctrines. 2. Spiritual life—Tantric
Buddhism. 3. Compassion (Buddhism). 4. Sunyata. I. Klein, Anne
C., 1947– II. Title.
BQ7634.H657 1999
294.3'420425—dc21   99-28437

ISBN 0-86171-154-8

04 03 02 01 00
6 5 4 3 2

Front cover image: *Klee* from the *Malevich Keeps Good Company Series,*
    Henry Elinson, courtesy of Duke University Museum of Art
Back cover photo: Daniel Chenn
Designed by: Jennie Malcolm

Wisdom Publications' books are printed on acid-free paper and meet the
guidelines for the permanence and durability of the Committee on
Production Guidelines for Book Longevity of the Council on Library
Resources.

Printed in the United States of America

CONTENTS

Buddhist texts are, for the most part, written in a formal, concise style that requires amplification to come to life. Without elaboration, even the most fundamental terminology becomes abstract, to the point where the spinning of theories, rather than intimate contact with the basics of life, seems to be the aim. Despite the narrowing gap between cultures in general due to better communication and mutual economic dependence, mere translations sometimes do little to create a sense that Buddhism is part of *our* world culture. As Wilfred Cantwell Smith says, it is important to move from "it" to "they," then to "we" talking about a "they," then to "we" talking to "you" in dialogue, then to "we" talking with "you," and finally to "we all" talking with each other about "us."[1] This progression means not that we necessarily adopt another culture but that we arrive at the point where it can be seen as a configuration of *our* human spirit.

It is important to consider any religious system as a challenge to one's own thought, rather than take the culturally deterministic viewpoint that we are confined to the system that is currently prevalent in the culture of our birth.[2] The many religious systems of the world should be taken, at once playfully and seriously, as possible means for one's own development, not in terms of indiscriminate assumptions of what is merely different but of seeking to make use of whatever techniques are helpful for personal and social betterment. Techniques one finds in another system can often be used to enhance development and realization within one's own chosen system.

To do this, the ideas, concepts, and methods of various religions must be tried on for size, must be lifted above museum displays, must be confronted and allowed to resonate with one's own character. It is in this spirit that, after publishing twenty-two works, most of which were translations and analyses of Buddhist texts, I present here a personalized account of central Buddhist practices.

The book is based on two series of lectures[3] on basic Buddhist perspectives on the nature of phenomena, relationships between people, and techniques for gradually transmuting the mind into enlightenment. The first part presents practices that form the basic Buddhist path—realistic appraisal of the condition of ordinary life, the importance of compassion, and the wisdom of emptiness, as well as how to cultivate these in meditation. The second part presents the distinguishing feature of tantric Buddhism, deity yoga, whereby one imagines oneself as an ideal being, and its place in the spiritual path. In this light, tantra is seen as an integral part of the Buddhist path, literally a reshaping of the practices of compassion and wisdom.

The second part includes a delineation of the view of emptiness in the Middle Way Consequence School[4] according to the interpretation of Ðzong-ka-b̄a,[5] the founder of what came to be known at the Ge-luk-b̄a[6] sect of Tibetan Buddhism. In Ðzong-ka-b̄a's estimation, the view of emptiness in this school is dramatically different from all other Buddhist schools. He also felt that his own study and meditation had brought about a realization of this view unlike that of any other previous Tibetan scholar-yogi. At the beginning of his *The Essence of Eloquence,*[7] when he states his intention to compose this work, he says in reference to earlier Tibetan scholar-yogis:

> Many who had much hearing of the great texts,
> Who worked with much weariness also at the path of reasoning,
> And who were not low in accumulation of the good qualities of
>   clear realization
> Worked hard at but did not realize this topic.
> Having perceived it well through the kindness of the smooth
>   protector and guru [Mañjushrī], I will explain it with an attitude
>   of great mercy.

Ðzong-ka-b̄a's claim to new understanding serves as the basis for a new sect. The fact that just prior to this statement he pays obeisance to eleven Indian masters but not a single Tibetan teacher suggests that he views his lineage as bypassing earlier Tibetans and, in a sense, as being in a direct line from the proto-source of wisdom teachings. This is also suggested by his stated reliance on the god of wisdom, Mañjushrī, the manifestation of the wisdom of the Buddhas. As Gung-tang Gön-chok-den-bay-drön-may, a great late eighteenth- and early nineteenth-century scholar-yogi from Amdo province of Tibet, fleshes out the above lines:[8]

> Those excellent beings each possessed many qualities of clear realization of the vast path of compassionate activities; they each engaged in vast hearing of and thinking on the great texts of sūtra and mantra in addition to having highly developed intelligence attained from birth (due to training in past lives). In particular, each of them, wishing to investigate the essential points of the view of emptiness, worked hard at the path of reasoning without any sense of fatigue. However, they were not able to realize the meaning of suchness, which Dzong-ka-ba, upon engaging in purification of obstructions and accumulation of merit through very strenuous asceticism and upon analyzing the meaning of the texts, found through the kindness of the Protector Mañjushrī's taking care of him as his student.

In this book, I have not let a sense of ecumenism prevent me from presenting Dzong-ka-ba's unique understanding of the view of emptiness. I hold that the spirit of ecumenism, so crucial in overcoming bias, requires thoroughgoing but unpartisan inquiry. The need for friendly dialogue should not discourage the analysis of issues of difference; rather, it calls for disavowing factionalism.

Some have drawn the conclusion from my having published many books about the Ge-luk-ba order that I am a Ge-luk-ba myself, but I am not. I find it sufficient to be called a Buddhist—which is defined in Tibetan scholastic literature as someone who takes refuge, from the depths of his heart, in Buddha, his doctrine, and the spiritual community—even though I cannot claim that my heart does not often rush in other, far less productive directions. As the present Dalai Lama has said, referring to the Tibetan practice of identifying sects by hat color, "Buddha did not wear a hat!" I seek to draw inspiration and practices from all types of Buddhism, as well as from other religions and from systems of psychology. Seeing that Dzong-ka-ba's claim of unique understanding offers much food for thought, I offer a few morsels here.

This book was originally edited by Professor Anne Klein, now teaching at Rice University, who encouraged me to publish it because of its accessibility. In order to keep that openness, we have not loaded the book with technical footnotes but instead have given only general references to the translations on which each part is based. Reflecting the conversational style of several Tibetan teachers who made the topics of enlightenment come alive for me as in a grand story, the book presents aspects of the journey to enlightenment much like mapping the road to a marvelous city of the spiritual imagination.

Jeffrey Hopkins
University of Virginia

ACKNOWLEDGMENTS

Over the past thirty-seven years I have had the good fortune to study with eighteen Tibetan and Mongolian lamas. Six are from the Go-mang College of Dre-bung Monastic University in Hla-ṣa: the late Geshe Wangyal (a Kalmuck Mongolian scholar-adept from Astrakhan, Russia); the late Geshe Kalden from Inner Mongolia; the late Kensur Ngawang Lekden (former abbot of the Tantric College of Lower Hla-ṣa); the late Geshe Gedün Lodrö (professor at the University of Hamburg); Geshe Thupten Gyatso, treasurer of the college; and Gen Tenzin, an Inner Mongolian and likely the last great Mongolian scholar in Tibet. Five are from the Lo-sel-ling College of Dre-bung Monastic University: the late Kensur Yeshi Thupten, one-time abbot of that college; Denma Lochö Rinbochay, abbot of a small monastery in Kulu, India, and later abbot of the Dalai Lama's own Namgyal Monastery in Dharamsala; Gen Losang Gyatso, principal of the Buddhist School of Dialectics in Dharamsala, North India, until his recent murder;[9] Geshe Palden Drakpa, a senior teacher at the college; and Geshe Yeshe Thabkhe, a teacher at the Institute of Higher Tibetan Studies in Sarnath. Two are from the Jay College of Ṣe-ra Monastic University: Geshe Lhundup Sopa, a retired professor from the University of Wisconsin, and the late Geshe Tadrin Rabten, abbot of a monastery in Mount Pelerin, Switzerland. Two are from the East Point College of Gan-den Monastic University: Lati Rinbochay, one-time abbot of the college, and Konchok Tsering, the current abbot. The late Jampel Shenpen Rinbochay, from the North Point College of Gan-den Monastic University, was abbot of the Tantric College of Lower Hla-ṣa when it relocated to South India and became the "throne holder," that is, the head, of the Ge-luk-ba order. Khetsun Sangpo Rinbochay of the Ñying-ma order is the founder of a monastery in Boda, Nepal, and a retreat center in the hills outside Boda. Of great importance has been His Holiness the Dalai Lama, who has urged and helped me into several new fields of study. Simply put, these lamas' intimate and vivid portrayals of Buddhist practice, psychology, and philosophy made this book possible.

The opportunity to meet these scholar-yogis was provided by Fulbright grants in 1972 and 1982, grants from the American Institute of Indian Studies in 1979 and 1981, and several grants from the University of Virginia—allowing ten research trips to India. I have made five research trips to Tibet on an informal basis. Also, the Ellan Bayard Weedon Foundation and the Center for South Asian Studies at the University of Virginia have provided funds since 1974 for visiting Tibetan scholars, thereby facilitating joint projects with several of the scholars listed above.

I would like to thank Dr. Gareth Sparham for typing the entire original manuscript and Dr. Elizabeth Napper for reading it and making copious suggestions.

TECHNICAL NOTE

The names of Tibetan authors and orders are given in "essay pho-netics" for the sake of easy pronunciation; for a discussion of the system used, see the technical note at the beginning of my *Meditation on Emptiness* (London: Wisdom, 1983; revised edition, Boston: Wisdom, 1996), pp. 19–22. This system is used consistently (except in the acknowledgments), with the result that a few well-known names are rendered differently: for example, "Lhasa" is rendered as "Hla-śa," since the letter "h" is pronounced before the letter "l." Transliteration of Tibetan is done in accordance with a system devised by Turrell Wylie; see "A Standard System of Tibetan Transcription," *Harvard Journal of Asiatic Studies* 22 (1959): 261–67. For the names of Indian scholars and systems used in the body of the text, *ch, sh,* and *ṣh* are used instead of the more usual *c, ś,* and *ṣ* for the sake of easy pronun-ciation by non-specialists; however, *chchh* is not used for *cch*. In the notes the usual transliteration system for Sanskrit is used.

PART ONE

The Basic Path

Based on

Tantric Practice in Nyingma

Compassion in Tibetan Buddhism

Cutting through Appearances:
The Practice and Theory of Tibetan Buddhism

Meditation on Emptiness

and

Emptiness Yoga

1. NIRVĀṆA

Nirvāṇa is an extinguishment of desire, hatred, and ignorance that is often likened to the dying of a flame. Since ignorance is the fuel or source of both desire and hatred, the primary task in achieving nirvāṇa is to remove ignorance. Nirvāṇa was translated from Sanskrit into Tibetan as "passed beyond sorrow" *(mya ngan las 'das pa),* and sorrow is identified as the afflictive emotions of desire, hatred, and ignorance, as well as the sufferings produced by them. In that the chief of these is ignorance, the essential meaning of nirvāṇa is "passed beyond ignorance."

Ignorance is a consciousness that conceives inherent or pointable concrete existence in persons and other things. It is not a mere lack of knowledge about reality but an erroneous conception about the way phenomena exist. A lack of knowledge would be, for instance, a governor's not knowing how many people live in his or her state; an erroneous conception would be the conviction that the state contains three hundred and fifty thousand people when it actually contains two million. The latter is quite different from a simple lack of knowledge.

The ignorance that is the root of suffering is a conception discordant with reality, held with enormous conviction. We are convinced that persons and other phenomena exist as solid, concrete, or self-propelled units because that is how they appear to us. Yet this appearance is thoroughly deceptive, for people and things do not exist this way at all. Nonetheless, through our own ignorance we assent to their false appearance and base most of our lives on this misconception.

In order to attain nirvāṇa, we must first understand how things actually exist and then become accustomed to that understanding so that neither the manifest nor dormant forms of ignorance remain or can reoccur. The mind must be transformed, and transformation of such a magnitude requires great effort and meditation.

According to the Mind-Only School *(sems tsam pa, cittamātra)*, one aspect of the false appearance of things is the appearance of subject and object such that the subject seems to be utterly cut off from the object. In a sense, looking at another person or object is like looking across a chasm. The subject "I" seems to be distant and cut off from the object "you" or "it," as if the two were irrevocably separate and independent entities. It is correct to say that subject and object are *different,* but incorrect to conceive of them as different entities, or, as is said in the Middle Way Consequence School *(dbu ma thal 'gyur pa, prāsaṅgikamā-dhyamika),* to conceive of them as *inherently established.* Of course, we do not actually say, "I am a different entity from you," or "I am a different entity from that desk," but such words are certainly descriptive of our experience. By bringing about a slight change in our thought it is possible to begin experiencing subject and object as not solidly separate entities.

Consider the following. A feature of our misconception of phenomena is that things seem to exist by way of their own character or inherently, almost as if they were not composed of parts. For example, this shape A appears to be the letter "A" *in and of itself.* The force of its appearance as the letter "A" is so strong that we feel it is foolish even to mention that it appears to be a letter "A" in and of itself. We feel that it simply *is* the letter "A." No one (at least no trained English reader) can deny that "A" does appear to exist right there with or among those three lines. Yet, are these shapes actually the letter "A" in and of themselves, or is the letter "A" something we impute to them? Is "/" the letter "A"? Or "-"? Or "\"? Certainly not. But if you begin to move the three lines together in the right way, at a certain point they seem to become the letter "A" in and of themselves.

Of what significance is this? When you have all the materials for building a house laid out on the ground, no one points to it and calls it a house. You begin to arrange the parts, and one day it comes together; after that it is house. The proponents of the Middle Way

Consequence School assert that if you were to search for that house or for the letter "A," you would not be able to point to anything and say of it, "This is the house," or "This is the letter 'A.'"

The process of searching for such things is not intended to lead to the nihilistic view that since they cannot be found they do not exist; rather, its significance lies in uncovering a gross misconception that has great influence on our behavior and to which we are addicted. However, our conception of inherent or pointable concrete existence is so strong that not finding a pointable object may cause us to feel, "If it does not exist in and of itself, it must not exist at all." We look at the shape "A" and think, "If *that* is not the letter 'A,' what is?" "If *that* is not the letter 'A,' there is no such thing as the letter 'A'!" These thoughts come from our conviction that the letter must be right there, that we can point to it with our finger.

What lies at the end of our finger? It is something that goes up, down, and over the middle. But the right slanted line is not the letter "A," the left slanted line is not the letter "A," and the crossbar is not the letter "A." Is there a fourth thing that encompasses all three of these lines that is the letter "A"? When you build a house, is there a thing in addition to all the parts that spreads through those parts and *is* the house?

Look at a cement block. You think, "If this is not a cement block, what is it?" But look at it carefully. The little grain of sand you see in the corner is not the cement block, this one on the side is not the cement block, and this one over on the other corner is not the cement block either. You can come to the same conclusion with regard to every single grain of sand in the block. In that case, is there something other than all these grains of sand that encompasses the entire block? Can you find such a thing? You cannot.

This type of inquiry makes sense only when we recognize that we base our lives on the supposition that wholes exist spread over their parts, like mayonnaise smeared over a piece of bread. It is undeniable that when we are not questioning, when we are just living our lives, it does seem as if there were just such a whole, solid cement block. You do not say to yourself, "This cement block is different from all the grains of sand composing it." Nor do you say that it is the same as all the grains of sand. You do not enter into such analysis but simply think, "This is a cement block."

Proponents of the Middle Way Consequence School search carefully for this thing that is pointed to. They understand that the objects appearing to the mind and senses are like illusions in that they appear one way but exist another—they appear to be concretely pointable, they appear to exist in their own right but do not, just as an illusion appears to be something but is not. Analysis shows that this seemingly inherent existence is a misconception. There is a discrepancy between how things appear and how they actually exist.

The same unfindability applies to people, bodies, faces, and so on. Your head may feel ready to burst open when you realize that even though you usually feel there are such things you cannot find them when you look for them. This is one of the central topics of wisdom.

This does not imply a nihilistic view. One is merely washing away a misconception. This Buddhist position is that the information gained through our senses is false with regard to the status of the object and that by taking things at face value we assent to erroneous sense data. Our mistake is not a matter of having intellectually superimposed a false notion on *correct* experience; rather, our conditioning is such that phenomena appear to us wrongly from the very first moment of perception. We are deceived and, in addition, even build philosophies and systems of practice that fortify this deception.

It may be convenient to imagine that there is a cement block encompassing all those grains of sand. But does this view lead us into trouble? There is no question that we are often shocked by the events of the world; we would, for instance, be surprised to return home and find that our house had collapsed or had burned down. Buddhists say that such surprise is due to our mistaken view that the house exists by way of its own entity, by way of its own being. We have endowed our house with a false sense of solidity, which so deceives us that we are startled when its seeming substantiality is betrayed.

Due to our exaggerated image or reification of phenomena we generate attachment to houses and other items to the extent that we would fight viciously in order to possess them. Therefore, desire and hatred are said to be based on ignorance. When someone understands that things do not exist in and of themselves, afflictive desire and hatred are impossible. It is not a matter of suppressing desire and hatred; rather, they can no longer arise because the ignorance that is essential to their generation has been eradicated. Prior to attaining nirvāṇa, however, some conscious suppression is necessary.

Buddhists generally identify two types of nirvāṇa. One is the nirvāṇa of a foe destroyer[10] *(dgra bcom pa, arhan),* who no longer assents in any way to the appearance of inherent existence. He or she has destroyed the foes of desire, hatred, and ignorance and thereby achieved liberation from cyclic existence. The other is the nirvāṇa of a buddha, who has thoroughly annihilated both the ignorance that assents to the false appearance of inherent existence and the false appearance itself.

The false appearance of inherent existence is like an illusion created by a magician who has cast a spell on the eyes of the audience. If such a magician created a beautiful man or woman in front of us, we might easily feel, "What a lovely person this is! Perhaps we will meet and marry. We could have such a wonderful life," and so on. We, like a magician's audience, base all sorts of vain speculations on the assumption that appearances are true. The magician also sees the beautiful man or woman, but does not entertain any thoughts or feelings about such. He or she knows what created its appearance, that there is no man or woman there, only a pebble or a twig that magic has caused to appear as such. While the audience sees the false appearance, believes in it, and therefore enters into afflictive emotions with regard to it, the magician is like a foe destroyer, who fully understands that the appearance is false and, therefore, is incapable of being deceived by it into vain speculation. A buddha is like a person who enters the room after the spell has been cast and does not even see the illusory snake but rather sees the pebble. A buddha's perception is totally correct.

Shākyamuni Buddha said that all his teachings flow toward nirvāṇa. Everything he taught and everything that present-day, fully qualified teachers maintaining his traditions teach is for the purpose of helping students overcome ignorance and understand reality. A teacher wants a student to become capable of remaining in meditation on reality so that by directly perceiving the truth of the emptiness of inherent existence and growing accustomed to it, the student will be able to cleanse the mind of all desire, hatred, and ignorance. His or her mind will then be transformed into a wisdom consciousness that in meditative equipoise remains continuously fused with emptiness. Eventually, it will be possible to manifest different types of bodies fashioned from the very substance of the wisdom that realizes emptiness itself; these bodies will then be used to help other beings.

A teacher presents the path in such a way that students are able to acquire the appreciation and motivation necessary to complete the path. Instructions are given on hearing, motivation, and the value of leisure and fortune in order to provide students with the information and background necessary to assure that they will actually practice what they learn. Teaching is not given for the sake of mere scholarship or curiosity. Its purpose is to help. The present Dalai Lama has said that if you determine that it does not help, put it aside and find something that does. If it does help, practice it.

2. THE JEWEL OF LEISURE

Life is extremely short. If we wish to hear about and realize the meaning of emptiness, the meaning of suchness, where will we find the time? Certainly it will not be easy, for our lives are so busy. Moreover we underestimate how quickly time passes and do not know how soon our opportunity for practice will be lost. We need to be taught that an opportunity to practice is infinitely valuable, for unless we learn to recognize this situation for the jewel that it is, we may neglect to use it.

As long as our bodies and minds are not incapacitated by sickness or stupidity, we have a good chance of success if we apply ourselves to the task. Yet, we do not realize the unusual possibilities that possession of a human mind and body provides. A Buddhist teacher carefully explains the possibility of being reborn as any one of the six types of transmigrators in cyclic existence—god, demigod, human, animal, hungry ghost, or hell being—in order to convey an appreciation of our own good fortune as humans.

Even within a single galaxy, the types of beings and the sufferings they encounter are extremely various; if the entire universe of cyclic existence is considered, the variety is inconceivable. Thus, the classification of the six types of beings is, if anything, a simplification rather than an exaggeration, but the accuracy of this teaching is not the crucial element. It may be that Buddhism is wrong in some aspects but right in others that are more important. For example, Buddha is reported to have said that the hells are located at a depth in the earth such that, if measurement were taken in accordance with what we now know the planet's dimensions to be, the hells would be located in the sky above North America.

When the present Dalai Lama was lecturing on the hells to a large audience of lay people and monastics in India in 1972, he asked the younger among them if they felt badly when they discovered that Buddha did not measure correctly. He said that such unease was out of place. We do not celebrate Buddha as a land surveyor or maker of maps. Moreover, a physical journey is not required in order to reach the hells; they can be experienced right here as one is dying. The Dalai Lama said that what matters is whether Buddha was right about the four noble truths, the two truths, and the like.

Among the six types of transmigrators, humans are in the best position to learn and achieve the paths leading to nirvāṇa. Students are taught to recognize clearly the features of non-human rebirth and the overwhelming difficulties that such rebirth entails in terms of successful practice. It is not simply that the suffering experienced by hell beings, hungry ghosts, and animals is great; for if one falls into a low rebirth, it is difficult (though not impossible) to attain a higher rebirth afterward. One does not acquire much new non-virtuous power as an animal, or as a hungry ghost or hell being. The force that has caused one to be reborn thus, like the force that impels a dream, is eventually consumed, and one is reborn elsewhere. Thus, just as a beautiful dream may follow a nightmare, it is not impossible to achieve a favorable rebirth after an unfavorable one. Also, although it is difficult for beings in a lower transmigration to engage in virtue, it is not impossible. It is said that there have been cases where animals, hungry ghosts, and hell beings have newly generated love and compassion.

If you perceive your fortune in having attained a human birth but do nothing about it, you are like a miser who, knowing the value of his or her gold, counts it and gloats over it but does not use it. If you pride yourself on having the qualities of leisure and fortune but do not engage in practice, you are wasting your greatest wealth.

You may prefer to think of the six types of transmigrators simply as metaphors for varying human conditions, but though this thought is helpful, it is not the Buddhist teaching. Students are meant to understand the hells and other transmigrations literally; they are taught to reflect on these sufferings as if they themselves were undergoing them. One meditates on them in great detail for the sake of incorporating specific types of suffering into one's own experience. This helps to integrate the personality.

Anyone who has vivid dreams should find it easy to believe in the hells because we ourselves often fall into a kind of hell just by going to sleep. However, we generally forget our bad dreams because we cannot incorporate them into our conscious minds. Similarly, when we hear about the different sufferings of the hells, we are upset; we feel, "Get that away from me." We must overcome this attitude and become able to face the horrors that we now undergo in dreams and may later undergo in a bad rebirth. These are not mere horror stories; they are horrors in which we are *already* engaged, either through inflicting them on others or imagining that they are being inflicted on us. For example, among the eighteen hells described in Buddhist teachings, one is particularly bothersome to me. It is the hell in which the force of one's own past actions causes one to be laid out on a table so that a worker there—who, like the hell itself, is merely a creation of one's own past deeds—can draw black lines on one's body and then cut along these lines with a burning iron saw. Perhaps this disturbs me because I mentally do similar things—make cutting criticisms and so forth—to others.

ATTITUDE

If the teaching of the Buddha is actually helpful, it is to your advantage to regard it as valuable and worthy of reverence. Buddha's teaching is rare in the world today and must be treated with great care if it is not to disappear altogether. At one time it was far more available. Books of the teaching are said to have magically rained down on the palace of the Tibetan king Hla-to-to-ri-nyen-tsen *(lha tho tho ri gnyan btsan)* in the fifth century A.D., although it was not until the eighth and ninth centuries that Buddhism came to Tibet with any force. From that time almost until the present—except for six years during the ninth century when King Lang-dar-ma *(glang dar ma)* attempted to suppress it—a continuous source for the practice of Buddhism existed in Tibet. Since the Chinese Communist takeover in 1959, the Buddhist teaching has almost disappeared in Tibet. Tibetans still living in Tibet may wish to hear the teaching, but, despite a minor revival after the Cultural Revolution, there are few lectures because the external conditions for doctrine are suppressed by an antagonistic government.

The existence of Buddha's teaching in our world is not eternal in any sense. Today it is very difficult to go anywhere and hear a lecture from a competent lama. If you do find such a person, it is most important to recognize the value and rarity of what you have found.

Unless you are moved by the preciousness of your situation, it is difficult to take full advantage of it. The simple fact of having time is precious. Those with children know how a child consumes their time for a number of years. A job also consumes time and energy. If you do not realize the extraordinary value of having free time, if you do not realize the precious possibility for the teaching or have a sense that our usual activities are useless, it is difficult to make the time necessary for overcoming ignorance.

The pleasures of cyclic existence deceive us. We long for riches and regard the rich with awe and envy. Yet, what pleasure does wealth bring to rich people while they sleep? For eight hours each day their riches are meaningless, and when they become ill, though they may call the greatest doctors, they suffer like anyone else. When death comes, their attachment to wealth and position only causes suffering. No matter how marvelous the memories of life may be, they are worthless when the body degenerates.

If we feel that past events or objects of pleasure are intrinsically pleasurable, we are deceived. Nāgārjuna, founder of the Middle Way School of Great Vehicle Buddhism, says in his *Precious Garland (rin chen phreng ba, ratnāvalī*; stanzas 349–52):[11]

> Just one by one there is enjoyment
> Of continents, countries, towns, homes,
> Conveyances, seats, clothing, beds,
> Food, drink, elephants, horses, and women.
> When the mind has any [one of these as its object],

Due to it there is said to be pleasure,
But since at that time no attention is paid to the others,
The others are not then in fact meaningful [causes of pleasure].
When [all] five senses, eye and so forth,[12]
[Simultaneously] apprehend their objects,[13]
A thought [of pleasure] does not refer [to all of them],
Therefore at that time they do not [all] give pleasure.
Whenever any of the [five] objects is known
[As pleasurable] by one of the [five] senses,
Then the remaining [objects] are not so known by the
    remaining [senses]
Since they then are not meaningful [causes of pleasure].

When an object of pleasure is not being enjoyed, how can it even be called an object of pleasure? For example, you may have a television, stereo, and DVD player, but when you are watching television you cannot listen to your stereo, and, therefore, the stereo is not an object of pleasure at that time. This may be a reason why things that initially appeared to us as inherent sources of pleasure are later discarded and new ones sought.

Also, if a pleasurable experience is repeated too frequently, it will cease to be pleasurable. If a thing were inherently pleasurable—if the inner core of its nature were to give pleasure—then that pleasure would never be exhausted by repetition or be subject to adventitious conditions. The fact is that we must manage our minds and bodies carefully in order to derive pleasure from our possessions.

Practitioners do not encounter as much dissatisfaction in life as worldly people do, and truly developed beings are beyond it entirely. They have a bliss that is constant and non-physical—the world is a show whose marvels cannot attract them. As Nāgārjuna's *Precious Garland* (stanza 375) says:[14]

If, through relinquishing small pleasures,
There is extensive happiness later,
Seeing the greater happiness
The resolute should relinquish small pleasures.

Would it not be foolish to forsake extraordinary bliss for the small pleasure of impermanent worldly delights?

The teaching of impermanence as a quality of phenomena is the cornerstone of Buddhism. Whether a situation is good, bad, or indifferent, it changes and soon disappears. It does not go somewhere else. The past is only a memory, but we solidify memory to such an extent that we are trapped into believing that things will remain as they are now and that there is a great deal of time remaining.

It is necessary to identify the sufferings of cyclic existence in order to appreciate how fragile our present situation is and what it is capable of becoming. Suffering is not emphasized for its own sake, but rather to point out a path that leads away from it. The knowledge that such a path exists makes it possible to face our own and others' sufferings.

If we can determine that our own erroneous conceptions are the actual causes of cyclic existence, we will realize that our attachment to them must be extremely strong. We can also see that it will take prolonged meditation to overcome them and that time and energy are needed. If this opportunity of meeting with the teaching is not recognized as precious, it is all too easy to tell oneself, "I will work now, earn some money, pay off my bills, and practice later on." If we do not have the time now, what makes us think we will have it later?

In March 1972 I was in Dharamsala, India, where the Dalai Lama still lives; he was giving a series of lectures on the path to highest enlightenment, each one lasting four or five hours with only a short break in the middle. The Himalayan foothills are chilly in March, and I had a cold. We sat on cushions, but after the first hour my legs and back began to ache. By the second hour there was no position that would relieve them. At such a time it was very helpful to have a strong sense of the preciousness of my opportunity and to realize that hearing requires patience and effort. If it were merely a matter of listening a little whenever the mood struck me, I would have left the lecture after an hour. With a little persistence, after several lectures I was able to sit for four hours without difficulty. Endurance and effort sometimes have quick results.

ENGAGEMENT

Buddha said that his teaching is to be examined as a goldsmith examines gold:[15]

> Like gold [that is acquired] upon being
>   scorched, cut, and rubbed,
> My word is to be adopted by monastics and scholars
> Upon analyzing it well, not out of respect [for me].

A goldsmith tests gold in three ways—by scorching, cutting, and rubbing it with a special cloth—to make sure there are no impurities. In analyzing the teaching, one should test whether it is contradicted by direct perception, by inference built on the usual sort of reasoning, and by other literally acceptable scriptures. For this, you need a playful attitude toward the teaching and a willingness to engage in it experimentally. Without these, you may be unable to gain even a glimpse of its potential benefit.

For example, you might resent hearing about the various sufferings of cyclic existence because you feel, "They are just trying to frighten me into taking up their system." However, it is difficult to sustain the energy necessary for successful practice unless you have concern for the future. For example, if I knew that I might have to move to San Francisco, I would be foolish not to consider what I might do if an earthquake occured. It would be helpful to learn about the effects of an earthquake and about precautionary measures to take. I could, at minimum, decide to stand under a doorway if an earthquake struck.

It is important to come to a conclusion about what the future might hold and to decide on an intelligent plan of action. Agitation is inappropriate because it immobilizes, but careful consideration of various alternatives is beneficial. If you were about to be sent on a sudden trip to Alaska, and if someone else knew about it, that person would be unkind not to suggest that perhaps you should look into what supplies and so forth you might require. In the same way, it would be helpful to be prepared for future incarnations.

Because we usually do not see death firsthand, we have to be told that we will die. Our immediate reaction to such a statement is, "Well, of *course* I will," but in an instant this thought has been replaced by a thought of something else. We wrongly tend to see our own death as something in the distant future. A constant awareness of death, of how easy it is to die, is important because it only takes one small condition to cause death.

A newspaper recently reported a story about a man and his young son who had just bought a new car. As they drove home, the car ran out of gas, and they got out and went around the back of the car to look. A truck rammed them as they stood waiting for help; the father was killed, and the son lost his legs. A horrible incident that could happen to anyone! What caused their deaths? They simply walked to the rear of their car on a day of joy.

Death is not final, however. The mind with its predispositions transmigrates and takes rebirth. Since the mind continues, there is definitely something of benefit that can be done. Predispositions that are accumulated in the mind go with it to the next life, shaping the environment and experiences of that life. Thus, effective practice that creates favorable predispositions in the mind is the one activity helpful for future lives.

Though it would be foolish to make too much fuss over external possessions or even our body, this is not a teaching to neglect the present life; however, it does suggest that the main emphasis should be on the mind that will transmigrate. Sooner or later you will have to leave everything else behind, and if you plan otherwise, you just deceive yourself. Plans and preparations for the future should be carried out with the understanding that they might never be fulfilled. Planning for a stable future will generally lead to disappointment, but even if it does not, where are all your past experiences now? Unless they have led to an enrichment of consciousness, they are not valuable in the end. Nothing solid remains that you can pile up before you like a mass of bricks; there is nothing like a bag of cookies that you can carry with you to nibble on. There is nothing but memory.

Nowadays, when you remember childhood, all the time that has passed since then seems to have disappeared so quickly. In another ten years, this year will be the same; the things of this moment that seem so vivid and vital will have disappeared. You cannot find the past, no matter where you look. But if you always act with the understanding that external things will disappear and that the precious opportunity to improve the mind will vanish soon, then whether your situation in life is such that you run a company or build roads, you will be able to reap a measure of spiritual development from your activities.

3. THE MESSAGE OF CYCLIC EXISTENCE

We generally have little knowledge of other people's suffering despite the fact that it is just like our own. We do not pay much attention to others' complaints, but when we ourselves are suffering, our sense of the acuteness of suffering changes radically. Our own discomfort can be used to foster an intimate knowledge of other people's pain. When you have a headache, it is important to recall that your mother, father, or friends also have experienced such headaches. Take the opportunity to realize that the pain you now feel is exactly what they underwent. Unless you are careful to make a conscious connection between your own and others' plight, when others tell you of their pain you will merely wonder why they are making such a fuss.

Human beings are more intelligent than animals and other beings, but we are slow to make obvious connections. Not only do we neglect the relationship between our own and others' experiences, we often fail to grasp the connection between different facets of our own experience. For example, we may be frightened for an entire night by a horrible dream, but when we awaken, we discard it as if it belonged to someone else. More likely than not, we take no account of the self who undergoes happy or painful dream experiences. We do not relate it to our daytime self; we learn little from our dreams and pay little attention to what they reveal about our mind. Instead we rush into the same pursuits that brought us into the dreamtime trouble.

In most cases we dream without even knowing that we are dreaming, and when we awaken we have no sense that we have experienced anything whatsoever. The mental continuum that is the basis of the designation "I" is non-physical and depends on energy, called "wind."

When we fall into sleep, the coarser levels of this energy cease, eventually giving rise to different types of dreams. It is difficult to retain the thread of awareness through these bizarre and often frightful experiences, but through practices such as imagining the lifestyles of other realms of cyclic existence we can eventually succeed in retaining consciousness in deeper and deeper situations. These practices open and integrate the mind so that its temporarily non-manifest tendencies cannot thwart helpful practice. Furthermore, by coming to understand the structure of cyclic existence and thereby developing a wish to be liberated from it, we can establish the context in which the practices of the Buddhist vehicles may occur.

Cyclic existence must be considered in terms of our own experience. We are capable of utterly forgetting past events. If it is true that we were previously animals and hell beings, we have no recollection of our past lives. We have forgotten our past so thoroughly that nothing prevents us from the actions of desire, hatred, and obscuration that create the causes for yet another unfortunate rebirth. If rebirth is true, we must not have learned the most elementary lessons of what to do and what not to do in terms of achieving happiness. Our obscuration would have to be extremely great.

Are there not instances in our own lives of long periods of suffering that we quickly forgot, after which we enter into the same activities that originally brought us such suffering? Are we that foolish? It seems we are. We are easily deceived and distracted by the appearances of the present moment. For instance, if someone you know to be a liar makes an impressive speech with apparent sincerity, the temptation to agree with him is strong despite your having previously encountered hard evidence of his dishonesty. You almost have to turn your head away and close your ears in order to remind yourself that the man is actually a scoundrel. Thus, on the basis of our own experience it does not seem impossible that we spent our past life in terrible suffering in a hell and have forgotten about it completely.

Consider also our birth into the present life. When we were born, we cried like a stuck pig. We cried because we were overcome by fear; we were moving, trying to leave the womb, wanting to breathe. We felt we would suffocate; our forehead felt as if it were being pushed down over our eyes. If we can forget such events in our own lifetime, it is not strange that we have forgotten the painful events of a past lifetime. We can minimally conclude that mere lack of memory does not eliminate the possibility of past existences.

One purpose of investigating erroneous mental conception and the process of rebirth is to identify conscious and unconscious activities of our own minds and to see the potentialities that are ready to become manifest. Also, recognizing the many varieties of suffering that humans and other types of beings undergo will enable us to direct practice toward all types of suffering sentient beings. Religious people are often goody-goodies who have relatively dull minds because it is hard to be both mentally sharp and compassionate—a clearly focused mind easily becomes damagingly critical. Meditation on the sufferings of cyclic existence is a technique for developing sharpness and compassion as compatible mental qualities.

In cultivating the bodhisattva path, you must develop a mind that remains compassionate in the face of any horror whatsoever. In making your mind open enough to face willingly the fact that sentient beings often undergo terrible pain, you are also integrating painful elements into your own mind. The process of integration can be difficult; you must descend in order to ascend; you must go down into your own horrors before you can integrate them into the scope of conscious mind. Often when we are deeply moved by the sufferings of others— as in times of famine or war—we bury our compassion because we feel that nothing can be done to alleviate such suffering and that it is thus too painful to have concern for such events. Bodhisattvas are capable of keeping others' suffering in mind. They are willing to feel very strongly about it even if they can do nothing for the time being to ease it. In order to help students manifest their own strong feelings, a lama often displays strong feelings herself. When told that someone has been hurt or when actually seeing an animal in pain, she winces as if hurt herself.

If you watch your own mind when you hear about misfortune, you may discover that a mechanism sets in immediately to block out whatever strong feelings may be ready to come forth. You may find yourself laughing at others' difficulties in order to be distracted from your innate sense of compassion. Why are we unwilling to face great suffering? We are busy concocting a goody-goody personality that is so out of touch with such facts that even bringing them to mind threatens the image we have of ourselves. Yet, if we learn to face these horrors without passing out—as usually happens in dreams—our minds can become strong; powerful compassion is then truly possible. We become capable of acting and directing our present lives within conscious knowledge of the sufferings to which we can be subjected. We can understand and come to terms with karma—the cause and effect of actions—because we have the mental ability to face the dreadful situations that certain activities will inevitably induce in this life or in future lives.

When you are able to face your own situation, you can relate to the suffering of others. You are open to the possibility of extending love and compassion to all the beings who abide wherever space exists. If you can do this, you will not be tricked out of practice by external circumstances. Goody-goody people, on the other hand, spend most of their time with other goody-goody people and are able to act charmingly with one another. If one of them sees a non-goody-goody person, however, his thin patina of goody-goodiness quickly disappears. He scolds the wretch who cut in line at the bank, for example, and decides that aside from his own friends, most people are intolerable. Such people remain victims of circumstance and conditioning. They have not looked into their minds and dealt with what is actually there.

The more we are able to get in touch with the unpleasant, violent, or frightening aspects of our own mind, the more we are able to bring practice into the depths of our mind. Practices in which you visualize suffering beings in the various hells and give them gifts that relieve their pain are techniques for gradually cajoling the mind into understanding itself. In some practices, you even imagine yourself in, for example, a hell where dismembered limbs retain painful sensation. Imagine your hand a few yards away and think that it still has feeling.

This can open the mind to the possibility of remaining conscious through an experience that would otherwise cause it to black out. By tapping the deepest resources of your own mind, it eventually becomes possible to turn all energies and feelings to bliss. But unless you are able to open the mind fully and retain a feeling of compassion for others under all conditions, the highest bliss is impossible.

A bodhisattva's practice is motivated by the realization that every sentient being in the universe, whether presently appearing as helpful, harmful, or neutral, is actually a source of help and benefit, for every sentient being is a field of merit or virtuous power. In order to generate the meritorious power that is required to realize emptiness and to produce the special minds necessary for achieving nirvāṇa, it is necessary to relate with other sentient beings; hence, to a practitioner, every person is a field of virtue. If someone is particularly unkind toward you, having a good attitude toward that person is like being able to plant the seed of a large fruit tree in particularly rich soil. Students are taught to be thankful to those who are not superficially pleasant toward them.

Profound gurus are not goody-goodies. They can scold in such a way that they appear like hell beings. If you have a special relationship with such a person, that person can use a pretended wrathful aspect to teach you to move the threshold of your own anger farther and farther back. You are motivated to lower this threshold because you know you must not become angry with your teacher, but when the guru finally pushes you beyond your "farthest" threshold and causes you to see your own anger, you know just how much of a goody-goody you are not. The guru makes it impossible for you to deceive yourself any longer, and you are thankful to him for revealing the nature of your mind. This is one of his greatest gifts.

It often happens that when you begin to succeed in stabilizing the mind a little, it becomes steady, but your perception is less sharp than before. As a result, you leave your daily meditation with a feeling of satisfaction and pride as a spiritually developed person. At that moment your guru comes before you, scolding, his face riddled with lines of rage, and from inside your own supposedly good mind curses and vile thoughts begin to arise. Thereafter, whenever you attain a bit of superficial stabilization, you do not conclude that you have eradicated a portion of cyclic existence. You simply think, "I have stabilized my mind a little. My mind has temporarily become stronger. There is much more to be done."

It is helpful to realize that each and every sentient being is a field of merit and that the worse people behave toward you, the richer the field of merit they provide. People who aspire to the bodhisattva path enjoy seeing other sentient beings. They feel a fondness for everyone on sight; a sentient being is always an object of delight. We, however, do not feel that way at all. When we hear sentient beings making a lot of noise when we are trying to sleep or meditate, we get annoyed. When bodhisattvas hear the sounds of other people, their mind lights up, "Ah, a sentient being," as if a little flower had bloomed there.

4. THE BODHISATTVA PERSPECTIVE

The Dalai Lama mentioned in a lecture in India in 1972 that all beings are always kind. Shortly after hearing this teaching, I visited the elder of the Dalai Lama's two tutors, a man who seemed to me the very incarnation of love. I asked him how it could be said that sentient beings are always only kind. He answered that all beings are kind because they are our field of merit—those in relation to whom we can practice helpful attitudes that empower our minds.

To my sight, he was a person who truly viewed beings this way. My impression that he possessed profound recognition of all sentient beings as extraordinarily valuable was so strong that it was almost painful to be in his presence. His magnanimity offended the part of my mind that wanted him to value me specially. I wanted him to think, "*This* is an intelligent person," or, "It is so nice to see *this* person." He did in fact appear to take great pleasure in seeing me; his attitude was neither neutral nor passive. Yet, I knew from his presence that his sense of joy would be equally great on seeing any other sentient being. He would recognize any particular positive or negative qualities, but he would not value people differently because of them. His valuation was based on something deeper than those qualities, and it was a marvelous teaching just to enter his presence because it required me to forsake a few baser qualities while I was there.

RELATIONSHIPS WITH OTHERS: REBIRTH

People who aspire to the bodhisattva path value each and every sentient being greatly; they can in no way muster a wish for, or take delight in, others' suffering. Bodhisattvas value even wayward people, because they are a field of merit. Bodhisattvas value them not only because they provide an opportunity for virtuous activity that furthers their practice, but also because of the kindness bestowed on them when that person was his or her own mother in a former life.

During our countless rebirths we have been in every relationship with one another. Through various circumstances the person who was formerly our dearest companion has come into a position of harming us, thereby bringing even more trouble on himself. However, the fact that his sufferings are the result of his own past deeds means neither that compassion is uncalled for nor that he should not be punished by society for his misdeeds. It may be necessary to punish him or her, but it is inappropriate to take delight in doing so.

If you feel that it would be impossible for a close friend of yours to become a menace to yourself and others, reflect on the fact that great changes happen easily. Simply falling asleep can create an array of strange ideas and extraordinary circumstances; thus, if rebirth exists, it must be easy to enter a radically altered situation after dying from this life. Furthermore, although it is possible to be extremely smart while dreaming, we are often remarkably stupid. Having fallen asleep at home, we suddenly appear in a distant country but do not question the situation at all. Instead, we accept the new scene completely and make plans on the basis of our erroneous belief. Our minds are so heavily influenced by error that we believe almost anything.

Like dreams, rebirth can quickly plunge us into circumstances vastly discordant with our present surroundings. Rebirth is emphasized in order to create concern about the sufferings encountered in cyclic existence. The practitioner is urged to find a means of overcoming those sufferings. Though some more superficial types of suffering can be avoided by moving away from conditions that cause them, in general suffering is not localized and thus cannot be avoided by going elsewhere. To avoid it, you must develop a mind that could not experience pain even if you took rebirth in the most torturous hell. This feat is possible because suffering depends on the mind in that it arises as an effect of our own deeds of desire, hatred, and ignorance. Desire and hatred themselves depend on ignorance. When ignorance is vanquished, desire and hatred become impossible, and no further suffering can arise under any circumstances.

The fact that ignorance and other defilements of mind can be overcome has far-reaching significance, for mind is what continues after death. Mind is not a physical substance. It is not composed of the building blocks of matter that constitute the body—the earth element or hardness factor, the water element or cohesion factor, the fire element or heat factor, and the wind element or motility factor. Thus, although the mind has a close relationship with the body, it does not dissolve or disappear when the body disintegrates. If you are able to ascertain clearly what mind is and if you observe your own mental continuum well, you will become convinced that the mind *must* continue after death. No one can stop the mind. Knowing this, you will regard your present body and situation as a temporary shelter, like a bus station through which you pass.

There are other ways to gain conviction regarding rebirth. Consider the behavior of young animals. In every species, not only do the newborn beings have desire for food, they know what they can and cannot eat. Why is this? Some call it "instinct," but "instinct" is a word with little explanation. In the Buddhist view, all so-called instinctive behavior is learned; we seek food now because we have sought food in the past.

If we remember to search for food, you may wonder why we do not remember much else from the past, such as our former language. Why can we not speak as soon as we are born? People who remember their previous lifetimes and recall how it felt to be born into their present life say that you do indeed wish to speak shortly after birth. You wish to do many of the things you were accustomed to do, but you find yourself with a tiny body, fragile limbs, and a greatly altered capacity to act. Your hands are now tiny; they may lie next to your face, but you cannot even control their movement. Talking, of course, is even more difficult; you may decide to speak to your mother, but you become discouraged because, at the most, only unintelligible sounds emerge. The difficulty arises not because you have forgotten what you once knew but because the nerve pathways and so forth in your new body have to be established before they can be used.

It is difficult to identify the "I" that is reborn. For instance, nowadays I am identified by the name "Jeffrey," but certainly the "I" qualified by being Jeffrey will not be reborn. The mere "I" that is designated in dependence upon the continuum of the mind is what transmigrates from lifetime to lifetime. The mind takes rebirth over and over and eventually attains buddhahood, but because of our misconception about the nature of the mind, we sink all energy into present appearances. The things we see do not exist as we perceive them; the strong grasping we invest in them causes them to appear as they do.

When we begin to train ourselves to overcome this grasping, we may feel we are drawing energy back from concretely existing phenomena. We have been so taken in by temporary, adventitious appearances that we do not realize them to be the entity of reality itself appearing to us as manifold creations. This entity of reality is the basic mind of clear light, which is continuous. However, unless you can actually experience your own mental continuum, such an explanation is mere talk.

If you do not remember your former life now, you may conclude that you probably will not remember this life in the next. The thought may then arise that concern for the future is unnecessary because experiences are not remembered. Yet, it seems to me that if you have compassion for other beings known and unknown, why should you not have concern for the "people" of your own mental continuum. Further, through becoming concerned for the future beings of your own continuum, you develop a sense that mental habits are what make it impossible to remember former lives. In that case, why not engage in practices by which you can gradually gain the ability to remember your past lives?

People who do remember their former lives usually remember until the age of seven or eight. To remember beyond that time is said to be an indication of considerable development. As the body matures, consciousness becomes more and more tied down to it, and this causes you to forget. If it is difficult to remain conscious during dreams, and difficult even to recall them afterward, think how difficult it must be to remain conscious during the experiences you undergo between lifetimes and while becoming accustomed to a new body. You do not necessarily realize immediately that you have died. You come to the dinner table as before, but no one serves you. You notice that people no longer pay attention to you and gradually come to understand that you have died.

The maximum length of time between rebirths is forty-nine days; the minimum is one moment. This time is spent in the *bar-do*, which literally means "between the two"—the intermediate state between two lifetimes.[16] Even upon first entering the intermediate state, you have a mental body similar to the body of your new lifetime. If you are not reborn out of the intermediate state within a week, you are reborn into another intermediate state, and so on.

Clearly, the bodhisattva motivation can arise in far greater strength if you have a sense of the inevitability of rebirth. For you realize that beings are to be considered kind because of the many times in the past when they took care of you. They have also harmed you in the past, but their friendship is more significant. It is like having a good friend who occasionally becomes drunk; when he begins to fight with you, you do not take it too seriously unless you are drunk yourself. You merely calm him and put him to bed. You know that, despite a temporary appearance to the contrary, this person is actually your friend. Similarly, since all sentient beings have been your mother and greatest friend in the past, you should not be overcome with anger if they rise up as an enemy now. Treat them as you would an aged mother who has suddenly become crazed and turned on you with a knife. You would take the knife away from her and take her to a doctor; you would do everything possible to restore her mind. You would not beat her up just because she attacked you in delusion. It is the same with all sentient beings.

People aspiring to the bodhisattva path feel related to all sentient beings everywhere in just this way. They care more about the sufferings of other beings than their own. They take care of their own suffering, but it is not their most pressing concern. The attainment of buddhahood is not their main aim either; their chief purpose is to help others. They seek buddhahood, which secures their own welfare, in order to attain sufficient knowledge, mercy, and power to secure the welfare of others.

Such people have understood that just as they are an "I," so everyone else is an "I." We often feel there are so many "I's" that we cannot possibly think about them; we are so overwhelmed by our own difficulties of body and mind that it seems impossible to attend to others also. Eventually our energy becomes so trapped inside that it cannot be turned outward at all. In order to overcome this tendency, a student identifies the sufferings of hell beings, hungry ghosts, animals, and so forth as a means of directing sensibilities outward. Such practice opens up the heart and mind, bringing an openness to the personality. You do not become incapable of recognizing your own suffering but, in a larger perspective, see it as less significant. You realize that everyone has such suffering and that yours is not special. You abandon the foolish sense that your small "I" is more important than all the others combined and thereby recognize that it is appropriate to emphasize the welfare of others.

People who seek highest enlightenment for the sake of all beings throughout space cherish others strongly. They train in cherishing sentient beings until they are able to replace their sense of self-cherishing with an equally strong sense of cherishing others. They train their mind to be free of the slightest tendency to desert others. When such people hear the teaching or engage in practice, they do so with the thought that their virtuous activity is extending help as if magically to all sentient beings everywhere. Meditators imagine that their meditation itself generates streams of warm, loving energy that flow outward and bring immediate help to other sentient beings in the area. At this point it is just imagination, but buddhas are capable of *actually* affecting beings in this way, and in order to become a buddha it is necessary to emulate a buddha's activities. Therefore, such practice can be extremely beneficial.

When you meet great teachers, you feel immediately that they are not like other people or yourself. Their energy is not bound up inside.

In every activity—in simply replacing a book on the shelf, for example—it is as if rays of light radiate from their hands and emanate many diverse activities that are helpful to other beings. A strong wish to help beings and a sense of actually engaging in the means to help them pervade everything they do. If they are not now actually capable of generating help in this way, they are training to develop the power to do so.

THE PERCEPTION OF PURITY

Buddhism can be divided into two vehicles, a Lesser Vehicle *(theg dman, hīnayāna)*[17] and a Great Vehicle *(theg chen, mahāyāna)*. The Great Vehicle also is divided into two vehicles, the Perfection Vehicle *(phar phyin kyi theg pa, pāramitāyāna)* and the Vajra Vehicle *(rdo rje theg pa, vajrayāna)* or Mantra Vehicle *(sngags kyi theg pa, mantrayāna)*. A practitioner who is motivated by a desire to attain enlightenment for the sake of helping all other beings gain enlightenment is a practitioner of the Great Vehicle. A mantrika or tantrist cultivates this same motivation and in addition imagines that he or she is a buddha living amid special surroundings and accompanied by special companions. Instead of entertaining ordinary thoughts about friends and acquaintances such as "There is that foolish so and so again," one cultivates the sense that one's companions are highly developed beings.

Whenever you imagine other people as greedy, hateful, or in any way despicable, these qualities become the objects of your own mind, and, in effect, you are mixing your mind with a low type of consciousness. Imagining your companions as extraordinary is, thus, a technique for enriching your own mind. It is not groundless imagination, for our present ordinary views of companions and objects are largely creations of our own thought. For example, a room fashioned from unpainted cement blocks and lit by fluorescent tubes is unappealing to us. Yet, if visitors from a poor country entered such a room, they might be filled with admiration. Their delight would belie our sense that *anyone* who saw such a room would regard it as we do. This sense derives from our misconception that the room is ugly in and of itself, irrespective of the consciousness that views it.

Until we recognize the mind as the actual perpetrator of impressions, it is difficult not to be overcome by appearances. When I first went to India, I stayed briefly in Delhi, the capital of India. I had just arrived from America, and Delhi seemed terribly dirty. The streets looked dirty, the houses looked dirty, and I suspected the waiters in my hotel picked their noses between serving courses—the whole scene was most unappealing, as if ugliness were inherent in it. After a few days in Delhi, I went to Dharamsala, where I remained for a year. Dharamsala is beautifully situated in the Himalayan foothills, but its roads seemed even dirtier than the streets of Delhi since many of them are used as public latrines. Due to this, when I returned to Delhi a year later, I was overcome with a sense of its beauty and cleanliness. I stayed in the same hotel and was served by the same waiters, yet I could not help myself from perceiving differently than before. Despite remembering my former aversion, I could not overcome my sense of pleasure in their appearance.

Through various internal and external conditions, we build up perceptions. People who are capable of practicing tantra work to overcome their erroneous perceptions by imagining their house, for example, as having the very nature of light. They cease to regard it as a thing constructed from wood or brick. Through this practice they come closer to perceiving the wall as it really is, without letting memories of similar rooms cloud their perception.

There are other ways of training oneself to overcome false perception. When students are taught that there are six types of consciousness, they carefully and repeatedly identify each type in their own mental continuum: eye consciousness, ear consciousness, nose consciousness, tongue consciousness, body consciousness, and mental consciousness. In this way they counter the misconception of themselves as single amorphous entities and develop an awareness of the many different functions that flow into their sense of "I." They determine that the entire array of objects perceived by the six consciousnesses can be included in six comprehensive categories: colors and shapes, sounds, odors, tastes, tangible objects, and mental objects. When the significance of this enumeration is understood, all diverse phenomena are known to be within the scope of their mind. Insights regarding the mode of existence of a specific phenomenon, such as its dependent designation, are then easily applied to objects from each of the six categories, and thereby their understanding is extended to all phenomena.

When the interdependence of designations—such as tall and short, high and low—is investigated, it must be done in a way that is genuinely significant for you. Take as your object of analysis a phenomenon that you strongly feel is tall and use all the mental force you can command to investigate whether that object is *inherently* tall in and of itself. For example, the Empire State Building may seem to be tall in and of itself, yet if you compare it with the two towers of the World Trade Center, it is short. As soon as you see or imagine anything taller, your original example appears short. If you begin to wonder whether or not it is only through a fault of mind that you conceive things to exist a certain way in and of themselves, search with all possible intensity until you become utterly convinced that there is no such thing as a phenomenon that is tall in and of itself.

In searching for such an object and failing to find it, one enters a spacelike equipoise. At that time the analytical consciousness discerns only the vacuity, or lack thereof, of such an inherently existing object. This vacuity is ripe with meaning: rich, dynamic, and vivid. There is no sense of nihilism whatsoever. Instead of striking against an object in the usual way, the mind is like a sword swung through empty air. Then, when one arises from spacelike equipoise, one understands all appearances to be interdependently established. One sees that tall exists only in dependence on short and that short exists only in dependence on tall. Having comprehended this, one should apply this understanding to as many objects as possible.

For example, if you catch yourself thinking that a certain building must be tall because it contains twenty-five stories and five hundred offices, analyze the stories and offices to discover whether they inherently cover their own bases of designation. Whenever you feel, "This *must* inherently exist because…," analyze the "because" to overcome your sense of its inherent existence. Eventually you will succeed in tearing apart your belief that persons and other phenomena exist in and of themselves.

THREE EXCELLENCES

A bodhisattva's every activity is conjoined with three excellences: (1) prior to the activity, the generation of the altruistic[18] intention to become enlightened; (2) during the activity, an understanding of the action, its object, and agent as empty of inherent existence; and (3) upon completing the activity, a dedication of its virtue to the welfare of all sentient beings.

The first excellence means that one enters into all activities with the clearly defined intention of benefitting sentient beings. Before teaching, for example, bodhisattvas reflect, "May whatever virtue I create through explaining doctrine help all sentient beings throughout space attain highest enlightenment." While actually engaged in teaching, they do not conceive the teacher (themselves), the teaching, or those who are taught to exist independently in and of themselves. They know that they are teachers only in dependence on students and that students are not naturally, or inherently, endowed with the nature of students but are so designated only in dependence on their activity of listening to a teacher. For example, if, after taking a job at a university, I felt that I had acquired an entity of inherent "professorness," I would be very foolish. I am a student or teacher only in dependence on whether I am giving or receiving teaching at a particular time. Could I shut myself alone in a room and still be a professor?

Since the teacher is designated or arises in dependence on the students, and the students are designated or arise in dependence on the teacher, which of them arises first? If neither is first and they arise simultaneously, how can it be said that one arises or is designated *in dependence* on the other? If you investigate this carefully, you will discover that their arising cannot be found, because two things that are produced at the same time, such as two stalks growing side by side, cannot depend on one another for their production. Therefore, even though dependently arisen or nominally existent teachers and students do exist, their arising is not a massive activity at which one can point and say, "There it is." Our sense that such a concrete, pointable activity exists, established by way of its own entity, is entirely mistaken.

In order to overcome this misconception and accord with reality, all activities should be qualified by a sense that the agent, object, and activity themselves lack inherent existence and are merely interdependent, nominal phenomena. This understanding overcomes our usual feelings that phenomena exist as massive or concrete entities that cover a certain area. Such misconceptions prevent us from regarding phenomena in accordance with their true nature as adventitiously arisen, like clouds in space. We foolishly pay attention only to the clouds, not to the place from which the clouds arise. Space gives rise to the clouds, and the clouds retreat back into space, but we are so involved with the looming shapes that we never consider the essential entity behind them.

The final structuring of an action occurs when you dedicate any virtue arising from that activity to the welfare of all sentient beings. This is the third excellence. You reflect, "May this be of help to all sentient beings throughout space." In this way the activity, however small, establishes a relationship with as many beings as you are capable of imagining. Such thought destroys the force of anger and allows you to develop increasingly virtuous, healthy states of mind. Due to a mistaken impression that the third excellence involves a sense of superiority over others or due to a sense of inadequacy—which itself is a form of pride—you may feel uncomfortable in making such a vast dedication. However, a dedication of virtue for the good of others creates a mental framework incompatible with pride, since everything you do is motivated solely by your wish to help others. When proud thoughts themselves are conceived to be for the sake of others, the sense of pride evaporates.

5. PURE APPEARANCE AND THE MIND OF ENLIGHTENMENT

The Teacher

There is an entity within us now that is beyond cyclic existence in the sense of naturally being beyond the afflictive emotions. We pay no attention to it, yet this entity is endowed with inconceivable potential for wisdom and compassionate manifestation. Instead of focusing on it, we throw almost all our energy into external appearances. In order to correct this misdirection of attention, a guru creates a situation wherein you must observe something other than external appearance simply in order to bear the difficulties of remaining with him or her.

Often a guru is an extraordinarily beautiful person to be with, radiating light and compassion. But sometimes it is as if fire issued from his or her mouth. When he or she pats you on the head and praises you for your kindness, you become extremely happy. When, shortly afterward, he or she scolds you and claims you have ruined everything he or she ever tried to do, you become very sad. Even after being shuffled back and forth between these poles for a number of years, it is difficult not to be overcome by the good and bad appearances of the present moment.

Ordinarily, we are unaware of our mind's tendency to lock into whatever appears before it. For this reason a guru must show us over and over again how relentlessly our mind is lulled and controlled by appearances. Therefore, a close relationship with a true teacher is helpful in gaining a rudimentary understanding of the conflict between appearance and reality. He or she provides an opportunity to practice not being overcome by appearances, for no matter what aspect your teacher shows externally and no matter how he or she scolds you or causes you trouble, you must train in constant awareness of his or her true aspect of wisdom and compassion. This training is most valuable, for if you are able to overcome your feeling that a difficult situation involves an inherently existent harmer, harming, and harmed, all things become bearable. If, after careful analysis, you find a guru who is extraordinary and in whom you can put great faith, he or she will be able to teach you in many different ways.

It is important not to conceive of your teacher as ordinary. Teachers whom you have analyzed and accepted should be regarded as buddhas themselves. If he or she has a flattened nose or a twisted ear, you should emphatically feel that he or she does not have such defects. Conceive that his or her mind is continuously engaged in direct realization of emptiness, such that mind and emptiness are fused like fresh water poured into fresh water. Consider that, through having attained this wisdom consciousness, he or she has become capable of manifesting a body fashioned from the very substance of this wisdom consciousness. By imagining that a buddha is appearing in the form of your guru, you allow the blessings of all buddhas to flow to you.

If you conceive your teacher to possess a wisdom consciousness, that quality will appear to your mind whenever you are with him or her. Through seeing that quality before you and mixing your mind with it, you will come to develop a wisdom consciousness yourself, whether or not your guru actually possesses it. The benefit you are capable of receiving from a relationship with a teacher depends on your attitude toward the teacher.

Our minds are devious; even if we are interested in something, we can be easily drawn off into other activities, and thus there are techniques such as offering *maṇḍalas* (spheres of offering)[19] that enable you to turn full attention to the thing that you have already determined to be more worthwhile than the other distractions. Maṇḍalas may be offered by means of a hand gesture or arrangements of grain that symbolize Mount Meru in the center of four continents (as an indication that you are pleased to offer your teacher the entire universe). Everything valuable that belongs to you or others is mentally offered, in glorified aspect, within the maṇḍala.

It is pointless to engage in such activities without having understood why practice merits your undivided attention and effort. Thus, the step of deciding whether or not the teaching is helpful is important. Your recognition of how profound and difficult a task it is to change your own mind will prevent you from proselytizing others. Practice destroys *your own* desire, hatred, and ignorance; the aim is not to collect followers for a particular teacher or for Buddha. A lama has no need for superficial "followers." The Dalai Lama once said in a lecture, "My stomach is satiated with others' respect." The person who benefits from the respect and offerings given to the lama is the person who offers them.

Gurus give students something far beyond cyclic existence or things such as money, food, clothing, and so forth. They teach the practices by which nirvāṇa may be achieved, and there is no way to match this gift. Although it is important to relate to teachers in various ways— serving them, offering them material goods, achieving what they teach—you must not feel that you are making an even exchange for the teaching you receive. Nor should you feel that your teachers are attached to any of the goods or services you offer them. The more you conceive them to have attachment or desire for such things, the more you will develop these traits yourself. Therefore, realize that you are simply providing them with a means of furthering their altruistic aims.

REFUGE

When a student knows how to rely on a teacher and maintain a sense of pure appearance with respect to the guru, she or he is prepared to take refuge in the Three Jewels—Buddha, his doctrine, and the spiritual community that upholds the teaching. Imagine that a vast empty space before you is filled with glorious buddhas and bodhisattvas. This is the same as mixing your mind with the pure mind of a teacher, for you imagine that each being is endowed with as many magnificent qualities as you are able to keep in mind. Each one, for example, is capable of bearing the sufferings of the hells without fear or pain. Picture several of them in a situation you know would be difficult for you, and imagine them encountering it successfully and with ease. In addition, imagine that your mother, father, friends, enemies, and all the limitless sentient beings are gathered around you, ready to accompany you in taking refuge.

After establishing this visualization, bow to the buddhas physically or in your imagination and take refuge in them. The beings you have visualized around you enthusiastically and earnestly emulate your thought and activity. Then imagine that the buddhas bestow all blessings and attainments in a rain of multi-colored light that descends on you and your visualized companions. In ending the session, visualize all those sentient beings dissolving into yourself and then visualize yourself dissolving into the field of buddhas, thereby becoming equal with them. In this way taking refuge embodies the entire path. First, you bow down to an external buddha, then receive his or her teaching and qualities, and finally are transformed into a buddha yourself.

After taking refuge in the Three Jewels, one does not afterward take final refuge in lesser protectors. Aspirin, for example, offers temporary protection against a temporary headache, but it cannot uproot the basic cause of the headache. Therefore, even when using aspirin, you should retain a strong sense that it is only temporary help. This thought will prevent you from being deceived into regarding it as an actual final cure.

The actual refuge is the teaching, or doctrine, which is divided into true cessations and true paths. A cessation is a condition of mind that arises when one is able to cease a level of the conception of inherent existence; it is a final absence of some portion of the conception of inherent existence in your mental continuum. True paths are not external entities but consciousnesses to be cultivated in practice, leading to higher states.

If your refuge is conjoined with the mind of enlightenment—the altruistic aspiration to attain enlightenment for the sake of drawing all sentient beings to their own enlightenment—you have the refuge of the Great Vehicle. Refuge merely taken out of concern for your own welfare yields little fruit in comparison.

The Light of Compassion

The image of a net whose every knot bears a diamond appears in the *Avataṃsaka Sūtra*. Each jewel reflects the light from every other jewel in many different ways. Buddhism teaches that our own mind and body can become related with others in this way. At present, they are so turned inward that they scarcely reflect anything; yet it is possible for them to be transformed such that they can reflect the entire universe. It is even possible to emanate a pure land from this small body.

One method of opening your mind to such a possibility is to conceive of yourself as related to each and every sentient being throughout space, including all beings you know or have ever heard of or seen in pictures. Since you are the one who has imagined them, they are already closely connected with your own mind. You can relate to them by feeling that when you bow to Buddha, his doctrine, and the spiritual community, you do so for the sake of each and every one of them. In addition, you can cultivate the wish that you will free these beings from all suffering and the causes of suffering. To this end you take a personal interest in everyone, in every form of life and situation encounterable or imaginable. This thought brings you into contact with countless varieties of sentient beings, for sentient beings exist wherever space exists, and space is everywhere. It is said that there are beings who exist even in the solid center of a rock; they have only mental bodies and are therefore capable of dwelling where physical bodies could not be accommodated. You can take refuge for the sake of all of them.

Many people who have already attained enlightenment are now working to help sentient beings. There have been many buddhas, and there will be many more; thus, it is not in fact the case that any single being will liberate all others. Yet in order to achieve highest enlightenment, it is necessary to have as much dedication and effort as you would generate if you were to be the sole liberator of all beings.

Reflect on a small area, the present Dalai Lama once suggested, taking all the humans in that area as your object of compassion. Then extend this to include the two- and four-legged animals in the area and then the insects. I would add that if you question the possibility of setting such a vast object in your mind, that very question means it is close to being in your mind, for the moment you ask how it could be there, you have almost imagined it.

We have become so accustomed to seeing things in terms of our own welfare—we are so turned inward and wound up inside—that it is sometimes difficult to open the flower of the mind and spread its light everywhere in the universe. Yet a bodhisattva does this eventually with ease.

It would be a mistake to think that the thought to practice for the sake of others depends on pride or that only proud people would care to cultivate the sense that their activity encompasses all other beings. We tend to feel that any thought to help others presupposes a sense of superiority over them, and this may make us uncomfortable. Even if it is a fact that some people are more advanced than others, when we know how quickly any situation can reverse itself, the thought of temporary superiority cannot elicit even a glimmer of pride. A student who meets with the teaching and reflects on it may decide that it is good or that it is better than other teachings, but he should not become proud when he sees others practicing other methods. He may feel that some others would fare better to follow this teaching, but pride is inappropriate. Therefore, if he recognizes that someone is training in hatred rather than love, he should simply feel, "This will bring that person suffering; it would be better for that person to train in love." Being aware of impermanence and the faults of cyclic existence frees one from pride. When you know how easy it is to die and when you recognize that the time of death is indefinite, you realize that no matter how superior your present condition is, it can vanish in a moment.

Another antidote to pride is an understanding of the nature of oneself, of emptiness. A bodhisattva who has realized emptiness understands fully that if she searches analytically for a self, she will not find it and thus makes an effort to remain in this understanding continuously. She knows that nominally existent people and phenomena appear and function, but she also knows that not one of them would bear analysis. How can she be proud?

With such understanding, even if all the numberless beings whom you seek to help should turn toward you and praise you for making an effort for their sake, you would not become proud. Since every facet of your activity is generated for the sake of others, the very act of receiving respect is understood as being for their sake.

The Sanskrit word for the altruistic intention to become enlightened, or mind of enlightenment, is *bodhichitta*. *Bodhi* means enlightenment; *chitta* means mind. There are two types of bodhichitta, conventional and ultimate. Conventional bodhichitta, as I have already mentioned, is the altruistic aspiration to attain highest enlightenment—the non-abiding nirvāṇa of a buddha—for the sake of other sentient beings. Ultimate bodhichitta, or the ultimate mind of enlightenment, is the wisdom consciousness of a bodhisattva who is realizing emptiness directly.

The aim of bodhisattvas is the welfare, or enlightenment, of all sentient beings throughout space. The means of achieving this goal is their own attainment of enlightenment. Consequently, although people with this motivation seek their own enlightenment, it is not their main purpose, which is the welfare of other beings.

Conventional bodhichitta is divided into two types—aspirational and practical. The first is the mere wish, aspiration, or intention to achieve highest enlightenment for the sake of all beings, which is induced by love and compassion. Practical bodhichitta is the mind of someone actually training in the bodhisattva deeds of the six perfections: giving, ethics, patience, effort, concentration, and wisdom. One engages in these deeds in order to carry out the aspirational mind of enlightenment. You do not have to be an actual bodhisattva to work at training in the bodhisattva deeds.

One becomes an actual bodhisattva as soon as one develops an altruistic intention to become enlightened. The first moment of achieving a fully qualified aspiration is the initial moment of the path of accumulation, the first of the five bodhisattva paths. By practicing the bodhisattva deeds and thereby accumulating great meritorious power as well as developing a calm abiding *(zhi gnas, śamatha)* of the mind and conjoining this with analysis of the nature of phenomena, bodhisattvas gradually develop special insight *(lhag mthong, vipaśyanā)* into the emptiness of inherent existence. They thus pass on to the second bodhisattva path, the path of preparation. Among other meritorious activities, the bodhisattva cultivates the view of emptiness even more and with direct perception of emptiness attains the third path, the path of seeing. For the first time in one's entire continuum of lives, one has direct and vivid realization of emptiness. With this realization one attains an ultimate mind of enlightenment. On the fourth path, the path of meditation, one trains in the repeated direct realization of emptiness, thereby becoming increasingly accustomed to it. "Meditation" means simply becoming familiar with a special object or type of mind. It is necessary to familiarize oneself with the view of emptiness in order to overcome the innate tendency to agree with the false mode of appearance of things and to overcome the factors that cause phenomena to appear in a false aspect. When these two tendencies have been utterly overcome such that they can never appear again, one has reached the path of no more learning: buddhahood.

6. GENERATING THE MIND OF ENLIGHTENMENT IN MEDITATION

The altruistic intention to become enlightened in order to help all sentient beings throughout space achieve their own highest enlightenment is not to be thought of as a quality that one reaches out for and draws into oneself. It develops inside. Everything from the very core of the heart, the very marrow of the bones, is *trained* to be other-directed. At present, the mind is hampered and stuck onto itself, but the practice of altruism can free it.

EQUANIMITY

The sevenfold quintessential instructions of cause and effect are a series of seven meditations that culminate in the actual generation of an altruistic intention to become enlightened for the sake of other beings. The way must be made smooth for this practice through appropriate mental preparation, just as a wall must be made level and smooth before it can serve as the proper foundation for a mural or as a field must be made level before planting seed. This is done by developing equanimity toward all sentient beings.

Cultivating equanimity does not mean that one strives to become indifferent toward all beings. The equanimity developed in preparation for the cultivation of the seven quintessential instructions extinguishes the desire, hatred, and indifference we presently feel toward different types of beings. At the least, equanimity must be developed to the extent that coarse desire and hatred do not arise when we encounter beings who were formerly objects of these mental poisons. It is also important to overcome the sense that some beings should be abandoned and forgotten about. When we read in the newspaper that an unknown person has died, for example, we pass over it. Such indifference or neutrality disrupts equanimity as much as desire and hatred.

Equanimity is cultivated through reflecting on the fact that neutral people, friends, and enemies from their side *equally* want happiness and do not want suffering. It is a potent realization that may seem obvious but runs counter to our failure to perceive and feel any sort of equality among these three types of beings. From our own point of view, since all three types of beings have *equally* been our friends, enemies, and neutral people in former lifetimes, it is unsuitable to hold certain people one-pointedly as only friend, enemy, or neutral and, based on that, generate desire, hatred, or indifference. It cannot be over-emphasized that these two reflections, though easy to explain, are difficult to achieve and require long, patient meditation.

1 Recognition of All Beings as Mothers

The first of the seven quintessential instructions of cause and effect is to realize that each and every sentient being throughout space has been your own mother numerous times in the past. In actual fact, the instances are infinite, but for the sake of a more accessible object of meditation you may take into account just a small number of past relationships with each sentient being. Reflect that any given being has been your mother, father, husband, wife, or closest friend many, many times and that, therefore, this being has an extremely close relationship with you.

We do occasionally experience a strong sense of familiarity with people whom we have just met. When I was in kindergarten, I met a girl to whom I responded in this way. Yet, if I met her today, I would probably not recognize her. I might feel that she was just another person. But if someone who knew us both stepped forward and said, "Jeffrey, this is Mary Lou," I would instantly recall the close relationship that existed before.

The first step in developing an altruistic intention to become enlightened is the same. Right now we feel we are surrounded by many people whom we do not know, or, if we do know them, we feel they are unsuitable and we do not care to pursue the relationship. Yet, all people—the strangers and the despised ones included—have been your own mother. When you were that person's child, you regarded her with the same consideration and kindness that you gave your own mother in this life. No matter how difficult you may find it to get along with her now, you would certainly never physically harm her. Even if she became temporarily crazed and attacked you with a knife, you would avoid harming her. You would console her and take whatever measures were necessary to bring her back to normal. You would not punish her for her sickness. The situation with other sentient beings is precisely the same. If they come toward you with anger now, it is because they have gone mad with desire, hatred, and ignorance. They have forgotten that you were their own dear child, and you have forgotten also.

Our relationships with one another are not frozen into a mold or limited to a single lifetime. Relationships are subject to continuous change and should be viewed in this perspective. Therefore, a student is instructed to imagine the transformation of relationships over a number of lifetimes. Reflect that you died in a former life and took rebirth, and that before that you died and took rebirth. Go back one by one as explicitly as you can. This will extend your sense of presence throughout the entire universe. There is not a single spot among all the stellar and solar systems where you can look and say with assurance, "I was never born there." Therefore, when you think about such places, generate the feeling that you have been there. Think this with regard to any situation you hear about, read about, or are capable of imagining. Reflect very specifically, "I have been in that situation and will encounter it again in the future." This helps to bring everything within the context of mind and thereby into the scope of your practice. Indeed, as soon as you notice any phenomenon or situation, it already exists in your mind, but you may find that you often remove yourself from the sight of an unwanted circumstance by thinking, "That could never happen to me." One of my teachers said that whenever we feel we cannot stand a certain person or situation, it is a sign that we are already quite involved. We are the ones who conceive of it in this particularly unappealing way.

The reasoning that proves all beings to have been your mothers in the past will also lead to the conclusion that all beings have been your greatest enemy in the past. You may know someone now who would be pleased to see you come to harm; every sentient being has at some time felt this way about you. Yet, despite the fact that they once did everything in their power to harm you, you should train to view their former malice with the same sympathy and concern you would feel if your own aged mother suddenly attacked you with a knife. Understand clearly that such an outlook accords with the actual situation, for the hatred that others manifest is due to a long-standing craziness that consists of a person's being impelled by desire, hatred, and confusion into relationships that are dominated by these forces.

It is essential to remember that *every* being we encounter is someone who has been dear to us. We must retain a sense of dearness whether or not their external appearance and actions are repugnant to us. I once knew a person with a deformed face whose expression made him appear ready to attack anyone he met. All his life people had subtly recoiled inside when they looked at him, and, of course, he sensed it. When I noticed my own feeling of recoil, I let the impulse fade away, and the simple fact that I was able to look at him for more than a few moments made me his good friend.

Often when people harm us either physically or mentally, we reserve judgment of them until we find out whether the harm was intended or not. If someone spills a little coffee on us accidentally, we do not mind too much, but if we feel it was done purposely, we become angry. This may seem reasonable enough, but think how nice it would be to be free from the influence of other people's intentions. After all, it is our own decision about the situation that enrages us.

Buddhists do not value people on the basis of their intentions. Instead of contemplating another person's malice, they contemplate that person's buddha nature. It is there, and it is a superior object of attention—one that will be helpful to the mind. The buddha nature in each person does not vacillate with circumstance—an extraordinary quality when we consider that for the most part we are overcome by minor events. Great effort and a strong mind are needed to discover the deeper nature that lies beneath the various shifts of personality and appearance. One way to cease being manipulated by such shifts is to cultivate the realization that every person has been your own mother. Whatever the relationship with your mother may be today, there was a time when you saw her as something too marvelous for words. This love and closeness still lies deep within the mind, and it is important to recover these profound emotions.

Often when a child is picked up and placed on his mother's lap, his happiness knows virtually no limit. He has no doubt whatsoever about whether this is really his mother or whether her lap is pleasing. He simply enjoys the situation. When yogis become accustomed to the emptiness of their minds such that the layers of their predispositions have fallen away, their minds are released into the larger reality—the emptiness of all phenomena in the universe—and this experience is described as like that of a child getting onto its mother's lap. Such yogis are undeceived and free of doubt. However, if they had not first been able to re-open themselves to the joy they felt when their mother cuddled them, they could not have opened themselves to the joy of an even greater merging. Therefore, it is quintessential that the mother should be taken as the epitome of the most beloved being.

However, if you are not yet sufficiently familiar with your own childhood adoration of your mother to take this as a basis for developing compassion, use the example of a best friend. Using the object most suited to your present emotional situation, cultivate a clear awareness of what your mind is like when that being appears in front of you; notice how you are moved by the mere presence of that person. Then, picture a neutral person standing next to the friend, and notice the difference in your mind when your attention turns there. You may find that you wish to chase away the intruder so that you may concentrate only on your friend. Make an effort to generate the same sense of dearness toward that neutral person. Reflect, "In a previous lifetime, this person was my closest friend. Through the force of our actions we died, and now he or she has been born in such a way as to seem neutral and without any relationship to me at all." If you are able to use the thought that this person has been your mother, reflect, "This was my own mother who nurtured me in her womb and later looked after me night and day with deep love."

When you have had some success in extending the feeling for your mother or best friend to the neutral person, begin to work with someone you consider an enemy, someone who actively wishes you harm. If you have no enemies, recall instances of temporary enmity and use the person of that moment. Your goal is to generate the same feeling you have for your mother or close friend toward neutral people and enemies. It is an interesting psychological challenge.

Without a belief in rebirth, whether arrived at through reasoning, intuition, or prejudice, it would be difficult to enter into the above practice with conviction, but it can be done as a psychological challenge. With such belief, contemplation of your own and others' endless continuum of lives enables you all the more to view present relationships as similar to the adventitious proximity of carrot and celery in a boiling pot of soup. You know that whatever relationships you now enjoy or disdain will soon disappear and that they will reappear in a radically different manner. You could not become attached to the fact that the celery is now next to the carrot, because you know their respective positions are undergoing constant change. It is the same with relationships between people.

If this understanding is to saturate the fabric of your life, a comprehensive revision of your present perspective will be necessary. You will have to develop a steadfast mind that is not buffeted by adventitious appearances. For example, for most of us it is a fact that when we picture certain people or situations, uneasiness is generated. What sort of mind is creating this picture? We have of our own volition conjured the image, so why is our heart turning cold—what is the cause of our excitement and shaking? Through practice we can generate sufficient mental power to make all appearances devoid of at least coarse attachment, enmity, and abandonment.

2 Mindfulness of Kindness

It may be true that everyone in this great ocean of rebirth has at some point been extremely kind to us, but it is another matter to acknowledge this fact willingly. Our minds are bound by a fear of being controlled by others, a fear that if we admit their kindness we will have to obey their every wish. This is not so. It is possible to recognize and have gratitude for the kindness of others without becoming helpless in the face of their demands.

A bodhisattva is described as being under the power of compassion; the feeling of compassion enhances her mental continuum, and, far from being unwilling, she cultivates it with delight. Her mind never recoils or turns dull for fear of facing a particular horror. However, our minds tend to withdraw when we hear about people dying in epidemics, earthquakes, and famines, or any other type of disaster. We know of the suffering involved in experiencing such things, so much so that we cannot bear to become involved in it. In order to distract ourselves from such emotion, we joke about the situation or simply withdraw into a catatonic state. We are unwilling to give vent to our feelings of compassion because there is too much unpleasantness involved.

One method for overcoming this inhibition is to realize the close relationship we have with all sentient beings and become aware of the kindness that they have shown us since beginningless cyclic existence. Every step we take is a dependent-arising based on the fact that someone taught us to walk. My present ability to stand upright and lecture is due to my mother's kind persistence in teaching me to speak. She held me near her shoulder, and when I placed a finger on her nose, she said, "nose." When I poked a finger in her eye, she said, "eye." She repeated these lessons over and over again. Kensur Lekden, an abbot of the Tantric College of Lower Hla-ša in the 1950s, said that we would all be like bugs if our parents had not taught us to speak, walk, and so forth. If we are able to attend school or secure a job or make our way in the world at all, it is due to what other people in their kindness have done for us.

We sometimes feel that parental care is not a matter of kindness but obligation. Since they conceived us, they are responsible for our welfare, we think. Yet, if you reflect on the realms within cyclic existence and the various situations into which one can be born, you will know that through their act of copulation your parents provided a precious opportunity for a human birth that is superior to birth as any of a thousand types of animals or insects, not to mention hungry ghosts and hell beings. Yet, as if this were not enough, we seek to extract even more from them, and when they do not refuse us, we take their kindness for granted.

Sometimes children may be born to certain parents because the parents have harmed them in the past. As a result, the parents are now in a situation where their own great love for the person they formerly harmed gives that person tremendous power to hurt them. The vulnerability of parents arises from pride, for just as an artist may feel it is worse for his paintings to be criticized than for he himself to be censured, so parents often have great pride invested in the behavior and appearance of their child. A father feels, "My semen began all this; this is my child." For a mother the sense of possession is even stronger because the child grew inside her and was for a time considered as part of her own basis of designation, just as much as her arms, legs, and face. When the new child emerges from her womb, the mother has an emotional dilemma: Should she consider it as her own self or as another? She tends to regard it as self, or at least as something that belongs to her, but we as children feel our mind and body are ours and not hers. This serves as a basis for child-parent conflicts.

Even if parental love is mixed with pride and attachment, it is marvelous. Without the expression of such worldly love there would be no model for spiritual love. Moreover, without the care deriving from their love we could not remain alive.

3 Thought to Repay the Kindness

The third of the seven quintessential instructions of cause and effect for developing the mind of enlightenment is cultivating an intention to repay the kindness of all sentient beings. This is difficult, for how can you repay a debt to so many? It is troublesome even to repay a monetary debt to one or two people, or to return even a portion of the kindness shown us in this life alone.

Our feeling of inadequacy in the face of such debt derives from a sense that we are small and possessed of little power. But, at this stage of practice it is important to set aside thoughts of weakness and limitation and to develop a sense of being in contact with all sentient beings. For example, we tend to feel cut off from others, especially from those far away, not to mention on another planet, but this feeling is based on ignorance. There are subtle factors as yet unknown to us, the realization of which causes us to lose the sense of isolation that has contributed to our inability to help others far and near. Reflection on the possibility of overcoming our limitations can help open us to an intimate relationship with beings everywhere.

The Mind-Only School of Buddhism teaches that the mind is like a hard boiled egg that has been cut in half. One half is the object; the other half is the subject that cognizes it. As a result we feel that subject and object are concretely distinct from one another, but they originally formed a single egg. What caused us to sever the two sections? Are we disadvantaged by their separation? According to this teaching we are, and all Buddhist practices aimed at opening the mind and empowering it to stand intimate association with myriad beings in myriad situations tend toward some mode of integration of subject and object.

The first three quintessential instructions of cause and effect for developing the mind of enlightenment do not differ greatly from one another. Yet, in order to make certain that none of the ramifications of the thought of other beings' kindness is lost, a meditator dwells with great care on the different aspects of each one: recognition of all beings as a former mother, mindfulness of their kindness, and the thought to repay their kindness.

4 Love

The fourth step continues the progression of thought. It focuses on the generation of pleasant love toward all past mothers. Although a feeling of love might be thought to arise automatically during contemplation of the first three quintessential instructions, the meditator here consciously and with great emphasis cultivates a sense that each and every being is pleasant.

Falling in love involves an amazing magic. As soon as the object of that love comes into your presence or thought, little feathers of delight spread throughout mind and body. This is said to happen because of a compatibility between the *prāṇa,* or energies, of the people involved. For the time being, these energies act as catalysts to one another and draw each other out. As time passes, the energies disappear or begin to course in a different manner, and this particular feeling no longer arises.

There is no question that we do not have this pleasurable sense with regard to every sentient being. Yet, is it appropriate for our feelings to be so rigorously regulated by the simple presence or absence of a superficial quality of compatible energy? It will pass in any case. Moreover, people who seem unpleasant to us are seen by others as attractive. If you regarded even the most unpleasant people as your own mother, or best friend, in a state of temporary insanity, you would retain a strong sense of pleasantness regardless of that person's external activities.

This is a principle already well incorporated into our everyday lives. If you see a good friend in a drunken rage, you do not attempt to reciprocate his violence. If he tries to attack, you step out of his way and let him run past. No matter how horrendous his external behavior may be, it does not cause you to lose your sense that he is your good and pleasant friend.

The goal in cultivating love is to allow your mind to find this pleasantness in relation to everyone. The simple fact that any given person possesses a buddha nature and is a sentient being who was previously your mother is sufficient cause to find him or her pleasant. This is not to say that you wish to eliminate the possibility of encountering the other type of magic that is love, but it is important to free yourself from the condition of finding unpleasantness in others and being ruled by uncontrollable attraction and repulsion. It is not the case that when you succeed in developing a homogenous sense of pleasantness with regard to all beings, all people become the same in all respects. Indeed, once you find the constant factor among beings, you also can become even more aware of the factors that distinguish them from one another.

Some lamas teach that the love generated in accordance with the fourth quintessential instruction of cause and effect is simply a sense of pleasantness for all beings. Others teach cultivation of an additional thought, "May all beings have happiness and the causes of happiness." This might not seem unusual, but if you carefully and individually consider all the people you know—many of whom you have just seen in passing—and consciously wish them to have happiness and its causes, you will likely be struck by the fact that you never had such feelings for these people before. Your feelings hitherto consisted mainly of indifference, wishing them out of sight, or perhaps even hoping for their misfortune. Even if you cannot yet have a spontaneous wish for their happiness, you can at least artificially develop this valuable thought in relation to them. In short, it goes against the usual train of thought to generate a wish for others' happiness. It can be most startling to discover just how much you do not like sentient beings.

When I was a child, I frequently fell down stairways. No doubt this was due to my own past actions, but a more immediate cause was that someone told me it was childish to hold onto banisters, and consequently I had no way to steady myself. Nowadays when I see someone descending a staircase, I sometimes notice a tiny thought that says, "May you trip." It creeps into my mind without my being able to control it. Actually, I am afraid that the other person will trip, and this fear reminds me that I might trip. It is as if I feel that one of us has to trip, and as long as one of us has to trip, I am thinking, "Let it be another and not me." It is a subtle thought, and I have to take care to work it around until I can think, "May everyone go up and down stairs comfortably, without tripping, in all circumstances." My attempt to generate this feeling makes me all the more aware of how much, in some sense, I want people to tumble downstairs.

Any practice aimed at transforming unkind or harmful thoughts into salutary ones is an excellent lesson in the difficulties entailed in altering mental activities. Although we may respond with immediate delight to the teachings on love and so forth and be deeply moved by them, it is not easy to extend a strong feeling of love to all sentient beings. This is an extraordinary thought that must be developed with care and, once developed, requires that one take time to become thoroughly accustomed to its implications. This is the process called meditation or familiarization.

Practitioners aspiring to develop a bodhisattva attitude accustom themselves to wishing that others have happiness and the causes of happiness. Since the causes of happiness are the ten virtuous activities of body, speech, and mind, this wish is, by extension, a desire for others to develop the ten virtues and thereby be led into a realization of emptiness and the generation of full compassion such that they themselves will become buddhas. In this way they will gain complete freedom from all difficulties and enjoy uninterrupted happiness.

We tend to see people and other beings as epitomized by their present form and, therefore, find it difficult to imagine that certain people could ever become fully enlightened buddhas. This is foolish. It should be obvious that they will change greatly even within this lifetime; yet our conception is so frozen that they seem to be beyond the pale of ever finding happiness.

Certainly, merely uttering the words "I want this person to have happiness and the causes of happiness" is not love. However, since words such as these can induce love, meditators repeat this statement mentally whenever they see a sentient being. Eventually, love will be spontaneous and universal.

5 Compassion

The counterpart of love is compassion, the wish that all beings be separated from suffering and the causes of suffering. It is a beautiful wish to hold in mind even if you are not certain that such is possible. It is all the more moving if you amplify it with the thought "I will free beings from suffering."

Compassion has three aspects, or strengths of mind. One is the thought "*How nice* it would be if all sentient beings could be free from suffering and the causes of suffering." For most people this is a brand new thought. Whether it is realistic or not is another question, but it certainly would be a superb state of affairs. One comes to feel, "*Yes,* you *bet* it would be nice." The second aspect of compassion is stronger than the first, "*May* all beings be free of suffering and the causes of suffering." In either case, meditators relate this wish to specific individuals, especially those with whom they have a difficult relationship and upon whom they may have wished suffering in the past. Whenever your mind is distracted toward someone, take that person as the object of compassion. Take care to use as many *particular* individuals as possible as your objects of compassion; this is important because it is impossible to develop strong compassion for an undifferentiated mass of sentient beings.

6 The Unusual Attitude

The third and strongest form of compassion is the first part of the unusual attitude "*Alone* I will free each and every being throughout space from suffering and the causes of suffering and will join each one of them to happiness and the causes of happiness." The latter part is great love. This wish will change an ordinary being into a person of great capacity, with a perspective far beyond wishes for one's own benefit.

Why make such a wish? Innumerable buddhas already exist who are capable of appearing in diverse forms appropriate for leading the varieties of sentient beings to liberation. Why should you duplicate their efforts by taking this responsibility on yourself? One reason is that people are most effectively helped by those with whom they have a strong karmic relationship, a connection established by former relationships that leave predispositions in the mind. Thus, it is said to be better to have a bad relationship with a great adept than no relationship at all because interaction with the adept creates a connection whereby a close and helpful relationship can arise in the future. For example, one of my teachers said that Hitler, who brought tremendous suffering to millions of people, will be in an unusual situation in the future. He will have to undergo the dreadful fruition of his powerful non-virtue, but when he eventually becomes a bodhisattva, he will be able to bring great help to the many beings he harmed in the past.

Lesser Vehicle practitioners develop love and compassion, but they do not assume the responsibility of freeing all sentient beings from suffering, for according to the Lesser Vehicle teaching there is no possibility of accomplishing this. Followers of the Lesser Vehicle feel that when foe destroyers—those who have overcome the obstructions to liberation from cyclic existence—die, all their activity ends. They are neither reborn through the force of karma nor capable of manifesting themselves in any way. The Great Vehicle, in contrast, teaches that buddhas, who have overcome the obstructions to liberation and to omniscience, are capable of engaging in vast activities for the sake of helping sentient beings attain not only liberation but omniscient buddhahood. The bestowal of such help arises from buddhas spontaneously; it is their very nature to give it. This power makes possible the bodhisattva's compassionate promise. No single person actually does liberate all beings because there are and will be countless buddhas who lead sentient beings to enlightenment. Nevertheless, it is important to generate a strong wish to help sentient beings such that you would willingly do it alone.

At present we are like black holes, masses of matter that collapse into themselves and are so dense that they reflect no light and cannot be seen. Our own selfishness turns us inward to such an extent that it is difficult for others to see us. Our sphere of relationship is very small. Moreover, nearly all our activities are done for the sake of pulling more and more toward ourselves. Yet, the way to strengthen what is inside is to turn it outward; the bodhisattva attitude causes this energy to emanate forth so that what was once a tiny firefly visible only from a short distance is transformed into a brilliant sun whose light spreads uniformly to every point in space. Turning outward and cherishing others more than yourself secures your own welfare far better than any selfish method you might employ.

7 The Altruistic Aspiration to Enlightenment

When intelligent practitioners decide to devote themselves to the welfare of others, they examine their own situation carefully. They reflect, "I now have leisure and fortune; therefore I am in a position to train my mental continuum. I have many faults, and I do not know how long the opportunity to work on them will last. I do not know where

I am headed, I hardly know what I am doing now. I can begin an attempt to overcome my faults, but at present I am incapable of giving lasting help to others." They then investigate whether or not any beings exist who are able to give lasting help to others. They need to know what type of person this would be and what type of development would be necessary to become like such a being. They find that buddhas, with clairvoyance and innumerable skillful means, are able to help all sentient beings without exception.

To repeat: When practitioners have developed the full desire to establish all beings in complete freedom from suffering and its causes, they must consider whether or not they are actually able to accomplish this task. When they recognize that at present they are not able to free even themselves from all suffering, they investigate whether there is any means to develop the ability to carry out their wish to help others. Intelligent people pursue this question with great force.

In exploring the possibilities of their mental continuum they meditate to gain an understanding of the nature of mind. Eventually, they achieve a conceptual realization of the emptiness of the inherent existence of their own mind, a realization of tremendous impact, which is based on a rational and profound understanding of the mind's true nature. Thereby, they understand that the mind is not frozen into its present afflicted aspects. Its afflictive emotions are like clouds in the sky, capable of melting into space and leaving a vast emptiness that is not merely vacuous but is itself fused with a wisdom consciousness endowed with altruistic qualities. This is a reflection of buddhahood itself. Through this, the meditator knows that buddhahood is possible and that it is a state in which one is able to help a limitless number of sentient beings.

When practitioners perceive that they are by no means bound to remain in their present situation, they vow to attain highest enlightenment for the sake of freeing all sentient beings from suffering and its causes. This is the aspirational, conventional mind of enlightenment induced by love, compassion, and the unusual attitude of wishing to liberate all beings, even if one has to do it alone.

This altruistic intention to become enlightened becomes your motivation for the remainder of the path to buddhahood. The higher you progress, the more you cultivate this altruistic motivation. It is said that in the beginning stages of practice compassion is like a seed; in the middle, like water for growth; and finally, it becomes like a ripe fruit ready for harvest. The harvest is the unlimited, effective compassion of a buddha.

7. UNION OF METHOD AND WISDOM

Upon long training in the seven quintessential instructions of cause and effect, the thought to achieve buddhahood in order to free beings from suffering arises spontaneously and becomes a meditator's basic mode of relationship with others. This is the beginning of the bodhisattva path. The buddha lineage has been awakened, and later it will be combined with direct realization of emptiness—the two together bringing about the transformation into buddhahood.

In both the Great Vehicle Sūtra and Mantra (or Tantra) Vehicles buddhahood is attained through a union of method and wisdom. Method is the aspiration to highest enlightenment for the sake of all sentient beings, induced by love and compassion. Wisdom is the realization of emptiness. Although the trainees of sūtra and mantra practice the same method and wisdom, the type of union involved in mantra is unique.

In the Sūtra Great Vehicle or Perfection Vehicle one generates a wish for others' welfare as previously described and is thereby motivated to meditate on emptiness. If the original thought of love, compassion, and altruistic aspiration is sufficiently strong, its force remains during at least part of the meditation on emptiness, although compassion itself is no longer present as a manifest consciousness. For example, every activity of a mother whose only child has recently died is conjoined with the force of her sorrow; even when her attention is directed to other matters, her mind is continually imprinted with mourning. In the same way the mind that analyzes to understand emptiness is moistened with compassion.

When, after meditating on emptiness, you again turn your mind to reflect on the sufferings of sentient beings and their close relationship with you, your compassion is conjoined with the force of the previous understanding of emptiness although the cognizing consciousness itself has disappeared. Therefore, in the Perfection Vehicle, the union of wisdom and method is a matter of wisdom being conjoined with the force or influence of altruistic method and method being conjoined with the force or influence of wisdom, but the two types of consciousness do not exist simultaneously.

In mantra, the two factors of method and wisdom are present within the entity of a single consciousness. Here, method includes not only compassion but also the appearance of yourself as a deity, your surroundings as the habitat of a deity, your companions as divine beings, and your activities as the divine activities of showering beings with assistance. Wisdom in tantra specifically refers to an understanding of these pure objects as empty, that is, as lacking inherent existence.

Although the two factors of compassionate appearance and profound realization are in the entity of a single consciousness, they are not utterly one, just as a table and its impermanence are not utterly the same, although they are one entity. The one consciousness is considered to have two factors—an appearance factor (snang cha), which appears as a deity, and so forth, and an ascertainment factor (nges cha), which realizes emptiness. Roughly speaking, this is like seeing a double moon in the sky but simultaneously knowing that it is actually single.

The Mantra Vehicle is also known as the Vajra Vehicle, the vajra being a symbol of the immutable union of method and wisdom, the union of compassion for all transmigrators with knowledge of reality, or of compassionate appearance and realization of emptiness. In sūtra practice, when yogis gain conceptual or inferential realization of emptiness—an experience said to be more startling then being struck by lightning—only emptiness appears, the object itself disappears. In tantra, however, yogis retain awareness of appearance *within an understanding of its emptiness.* Their aim is a union of the manifest and the profound, the manifest being compassionate appearance and the profound being realization of the appearing form's emptiness of inherent existence. Therefore, method and wisdom are here simultaneous. This is called the yoga of non-duality of the profound and the manifest.

The union of method and wisdom also is based on the relationship between two types of objects, conventional truths and ultimate truths. All phenomena—people and other things—are conventional truths. The emptinesses of these objects are ultimate truths, so-called because, unlike conventional truths, they do not falsely appear as inherently existent to a consciousness that directly cognizes them. In both sūtra and mantra the two truths are shown to be compatible; both systems teach that an object and its emptiness are one entity and that an emptiness does not in any way contradict or cancel out the conventional truth that is qualified by it, even though it does contradict the appearance of the object as if inherently existent.

All phenomena validly exist conventionally but not ultimately; therefore, an understanding of the absence of inherent existence or emptiness of a phenomenon does not negate the object's conventional existence. Nevertheless, when bodhisattvas directly realize emptiness, conventional truths disappear entirely from their sight. The description of this experience might mislead one into thinking that phenomena and emptinesses are contradictory. However, the fact that for certain minds a cognition of the one blocks out a cognition of the other is not due to the nature of conventional and ultimate truths but to the mind's imperfect development. At buddhahood, when bodhisattvas have overcome the obstructions to omniscience that have prevented simultaneous realization of both types of phenomena, they are able to have direct and simultaneous cognition of both objects and their emptinesses. Ultimate and conventional truths are directly and simultaneously recognized with a single consciousness.

The simultaneous cognition of appearance and emptiness in tantra refers to inferential or conceptual, but not direct, realization of emptiness. For until buddhahood one is not able to retain direct realization of emptiness simultaneous with direct realization of appearances. The realization is called conceptual because its appearing object is an image of emptiness rather than emptiness itself. It is not mere words but a profound experience—incontrovertible knowledge of emptiness itself through the medium of an image.

Lesser Vehicle foe destroyers—who have attained liberation from cyclic existence—have not overcome the obstructions to omniscience, which are latencies or predispositions established through beginningless misconception of the nature of phenomena and which cause the appearance of inherent existence. Although foe destroyers have totally abandoned *belief* in the inherent existence of people or other phenomena, phenomena still appear to their senses as inherently existent. As a result they cannot *directly* realize the two truths at the same time. Although at this level appearance is incompatible with direct realization of emptiness, upon final purification of the mind at buddhahood there results a capacity to emanate activities for the sake of other beings within totally non-dual absorption in the profound nature of phenomena.

Thus, appearance and emptiness are not contradictory, and an understanding of the one is helpful to an understanding of the other. Just as it is not necessary to burn a house down in order to clean it, so it is not necessary to annihilate the mind in order to purify it. Defilements are adventitious or peripheral; the basic entity of the mind is clear light. Since the mind remains after all its afflictive emotions have been cleansed, the process of manifestation does not have to be abolished in order to purify it. It can be cleansed, brought to perfection, and then used.

In order to become a buddha, the addiction to phenomena as they presently appear must be overcome. Consciousness must be demagnetized. At our present stage we are overwhelmed and deluded by the appearance of inherent existence; we fall under its spell and assent to it. When we enter a room, we feel immediately that we have come into a *findable* room, which exists somehow spread throughout the floor, ceiling, and walls. In order to become buddhas we must eliminate this misconception and accustom ourselves to merely nominally existent appearances within an emptiness of inherent existence. When this is fully understood, we will gain the capacity to benefit others by means of many special types of activity.

In mantra, this ability of a buddha is imitated during practice of the path by substituting ordinary appearances with pure appearances that are qualified by emptiness. To accustom yourself to pure appearances you visualize yourself as Vajrasattva, for instance, and meditate on an effulgence of light emanating from your heart that enters other sentient beings and makes them blissful. Your doing this is not to establish power over them but to imagine giving them contentment by fulfilling their greatest desires. As a result, they cease to be distracted by desire and enter into whatever meditation is helpful to them. They progress on the path until they themselves turn into Vajrasattvas who send the same marvelous light back to you, and you receive it in the great equality of each and every person manifesting as a Vajrasattva.

Through repeating such a practice many times over with great attention and energy, actual purification can be achieved. At that time all appearances whatsoever—despite any apparent splendor or horror—are seen as of one taste, as the mere sport of emptiness. Buddhahood has been achieved, and there is a flowering of innumerable effortless activities that are themselves a union of perfected compassion and wisdom. These now flow continually to ripen the mental continuums of countless sentient beings.

PART TWO

Tantra

Based on

Tantra in Tibet

and

Deity Yoga

8. BACKGROUND

Buddhism teaches two vehicles of practice, a Lesser Vehicle (theg dman, hīnayāna) and a Great Vehicle (theg chen, mahāyāna). The Great Vehicle itself is divided into a Perfection Vehicle (phar phyin kyi theg pa, pāramitāyāna) and a Secret Mantra Vehicle *(gsang sngags kyi theg pa, guhyamantrayāna)*. What are the differences between the two main vehicles? What distinguishes the Perfection and Mantra Vehicles within the Great Vehicle? These are the main questions that Dzong-ka-ba addresses in the first section of his *Great Exposition of Secret Mantra,* which I have translated and published, along with a commentary by the Dalai Lama, as *Tantra in Tibet.* These are significant topics, because if one is to assume practice of any of these vehicles, it is important to know its place in terms of the whole spiritual system.[20]

The Sanskrit for "vehicle" is *yāna. Yā* means "go," and *na* indicates "the means" of going; thus, "vehicle." *Hīna* means "low," and *mahā* means "great." The Lesser Vehicle and Great Vehicle paths are taught in different ways by what are considered the four main schools of tenets, which themselves—in a different usage of the same terminology[21]—are divided into Lesser Vehicle and Great Vehicle:

BUDDHIST SCHOOLS
Lesser Vehicle
Great Exposition School[22]
 18 sub-schools
Sūtra School[23]
 Following Scripture
 Following Reasoning

Great Vehicle
Mind-Only School[24]
    Following Scripture
    Following Reasoning
Middle Way School[25]
    Autonomy School[26]
    Consequence School[27]

Each of these tenet systems teaches three vehicles of practice: Hearer and Solitary Realizer Vehicles (called Lesser Vehicles by Great Vehicle tenet systems) and the Bodhisattva Vehicle (called the Great Vehicle by Great Vehicle tenet systems). The fruits of the three vehicles differ: hearers and solitary realizers attain the state of foe destroyer, and bodhisattvas, buddhahood.

The Great Exposition and Sūtra Schools, even though they are called Lesser Vehicle schools because they teach only the selflessness of persons, have a presentation of the bodhisattva's path as well as of the hearer and solitary realizer paths, just as the Middle Way Consequence School has a presentation of the hearer and solitary realizer paths as well as the bodhisattva path. The upper and lower tenet systems understand the bodhisattva path differently, but there is nothing strange about the fact that, for example, the Great Exposition School and Sūtra School teach the existence of a bodhisattva path. For, based on the *Birth Stories (skyes rabs, jātaka)* in the Pāli and Sanskrit canons that relate the events of five hundred pure and five hundred impure births that preceded Shākyamuni's attainment of buddhahood, they hold that Buddha was a bodhisattva. However, they teach that among all the people of this eon, only Shākyamuni Buddha was able to complete the bodhisattva path and attain the fruit of buddhahood. That is why, although Lesser Vehicle Buddhism sets forth the path to buddhahood, it does not talk much about it. In its view it is appropriate only for a few. To become a buddha one must engage in the practice of merit and wisdom for three periods of countless great eons. This is too much for us; we are taught to take the hearer or solitary realizer path whereby, at the swiftest, one can attain the Lesser Vehicle enlightenment in three lifetimes. This is the path of the foe destroyer or arhan, which is often etymologized as *ari-han* (dgra bcom pa). *Han* means "to destroy," *ari* means "the enemy," thus a foe destroyer. A foe destroyer is one who has destroyed the enemies, the chief of which are the afflictive emotions. According to the Lesser Vehicle tenet systems, Buddha—by following the bodhisattva path—attained the same type of liberation that foe destroyers attain through the hearer and solitary realizer paths. However, Buddha had special clairvoyances, as a result of having accumulated merit for so long, as well as a special type of body. This is the Lesser Vehicle tenet systems' way of presenting the bodhisattva path; they do not mention the Mantra Vehicle at all.

The Great Vehicle tenet systems, the Mind-Only School and the Middle Way School, also set forth the practices of one who is a follower of the Lesser Vehicle *by path*, that is to say, with the motivation of wishing only to free oneself from cyclic existence. They do not thereby set forth the *tenets* of the Lesser Vehicle systems—Great Exposition School and Sūtra School—but a Lesser Vehicle path for people who, nevertheless, follow a Great Vehicle system of tenets.

When Dzong-ka-ba speaks about the Lesser Vehicle and Great Vehicle in *The Great Exposition of Secret Mantra*, he does so from the viewpoint of the Middle Way Consequence School. This is the higher of the two Middle Way Schools—the Autonomy School and the Consequence School—and is generally asserted in Tibet to be the highest of all tenet systems. In his discussion of the Lesser and Great Vehicles, Dzong-ka-ba is not describing the higher and lower tenet systems; he is explaining the difference between the vehicles in terms of *path* and/or *fruit* from the viewpoint of one school—the Consequence School, the final system.

Buddha is said to have taught the doctrines on which both the Lesser Vehicle and Great Vehicle tenet systems are based. He did not formulate these teachings into systems; this was done later by others. But he did give teachings on which the four tenet systems rely, and these all remained intact until about forty years after his death. At that time the Great Vehicle teaching went underground or, as some say, to the countries of the gods, dragons *(klu, nāga)*, and so forth, much as Buddhism in Tibet nowadays has been forced into isolated caves and mountains due to the Communist takeover. Nāgārjuna brought the Great Vehicle teaching back to India, using books from the land of the nāgas. He did not newly fabricate the Middle Way School tenets, but he is the founder of the Middle Way tenet system (or, more literally, the opener of the chariot-way for the Middle Way tenet system) because it was he who collected and compiled Middle Way School tenets, set them off in distinction to the other systems Buddha taught, and made a great pathway for their dissemination.

A vehicle is a way of progressing; it is capable of bearing one to a higher understanding through generating certain types of consciousness. This is the main meaning of the term "vehicle" in Buddhism; the use of the terms Lesser Vehicle and Great Vehicle to designate certain tenet systems is secondary. The three vehicles—Hearer, Solitary Realizer, and Bodhisattva—or, put another way, the two vehicles of the Lesser and Great Vehicles, are described by all four tenet systems. Buddha had four ways of discussing the three paths, corresponding to the four systems of tenets. He knew that the same teaching would not be helpful to everyone, unlike a quack who simply prescribes the same medicine for all.[28] He spoke in accordance with the predispositions of his listeners.

Theoretically, it would be possible to teach a single system, having many gradations, that would take everyone's needs into account; the Middle Way Consequence School system itself has many gradations. The difficulty with this is that most people are proud and only take interest in the highest teachings. The Dalai Lama emphasizes that sensible people carefully investigate whether or not they are capable of engaging in a certain practice and choose a level that is suitable for them, regardless of what might be higher. But for many of us, just hearing that there is something beyond our own practice ruins it for us. Therefore, it is better for some to hear just about that part of the path that is practical for them because, as the Dalai Lama says,[29] practical application is the main thing. Learnedness is secondary. It is best to have both, but if you must choose between practical application and learnedness, you should choose practical application.

Although there is a generally accepted hierarchy of tenet systems and paths, this does not mean that only the highest of these is the true teaching. A particular person's true path is that which suits her capacity and one which she can profitably practice. The others are not true for her, for it is counter-productive to be operating outside one's own capacity. Thus, even if you study all the tenet systems and decide, as most Tibetans have, that the Middle Way Consequence School is highest among them, it does not follow that this is the system for you to practice right now. Merely to take on the so-called highest system and think, "I know the highest system, this other person does not. I am superior," would be a case of using doctrine as a basis for competition. If you use a spiritual path capable of leading you out of cyclic existence to become more involved in the afflictive emotions of cyclic existence, what hope do you have of reaching buddhahood?

ALTRUISTIC ASPIRATION OF THE GREAT VEHICLE

The Great Vehicle teaches three types of aspects of compassion. The first is a consciousness that takes all sentient beings as its objects and thinks: "*How nice it would be* if all sentient beings were free of suffering and the causes of suffering." The second is a little stronger, for one has a greater sense of urgency: "*May* all sentient beings be free of suffering and the causes of suffering." Here one more actively wants it to happen. The third aspect is the strongest of all: "*I myself will cause* all sentient beings to be free of suffering and the causes of suffering." This is a very strong aspiration: One has the determination and willingness to take on the burden of alleviating others' suffering, even to the point where one would do it alone if one had to.

This is the Mind-Only and Middle Way Schools' description of Great Vehicle compassion. The Great Exposition and Sūtra Schools do not describe it this way, and it is this third aspect that, according to the Mind-Only and Middle Way Schools, distinguishes the Great Vehicle compassion from that of the Lesser Vehicle. Hearers and solitary realizers—that is, Lesser Vehicle practitioners—do have the first two aspects and thus are definitely very compassionate. Followers of the Great Vehicle sometimes say they are not, but this is only to indicate that they are not as compassionate as those who develop all three aspects of compassion. Nevertheless, they are probably far more compassionate than we who *aspire* to the Great Vehicle path. If the Great Vehicle lineage has not actually begun to be awakened but is about to be, it might be said that its followers' immediate potential for compassion is greater, but a follower of the Lesser Vehicle has more actual compassion at present.

The third aspect of compassion, called great compassion, induces the wish to attain buddhahood for the sake of all sentient beings. Once this motivation is spontaneously generated, one becomes a bodhisattva; therefore, although great compassion does not make you a bodhisattva, it induces the thought that is the mark of entering the bodhisattva path, that is, the Great Vehicle path. The achievement of others' welfare is the bodhisattva's main aim; the achievement of buddhahood is secondary and viewed as a means to achieve that primary aim.

As a student of the Middle Way School, you may study the three aspects of compassion and decide that all are worthwhile and that it would be possible eventually to generate them, but that the third aspect is a bit out of reach. "I am glad to wish freedom from suffering for all beings, but my own situation is so difficult that now I cannot conceive of overcoming my own suffering, let alone take on the task of relieving all others' suffering."

Sometimes people become frightened at the thought of cultivating the third aspect; they feel one would have to be crazy to generate such an intention. This does not mean they do not have the Great Vehicle lineage—it only means that there are obstacles to it. This is no surprise. After all, if we had no obstacles, we would all be bodhisattvas already. Thus, someone whose Great Vehicle lineage is close to activation is not necessarily one who finds it quick and easy to generate great compassion and the altruistic intention it induces, but a person who *likes* the idea of generating these. He or she may think, "No matter how impractical it might seem, I want to think that way," and thus seeks to overcome whatever obstacles he or she has to generating the three aspects of compassion. This is accomplished through long and hard conditioning and through meditation, until these altruistic feelings arise spontaneously.

There are people who temporarily are completely obstructed from developing great compassion. They can hardly bear to hear about it, let alone try to generate it, because they feel they have too much to do in taking care of themselves. No matter what is said, the Great Vehicle lineage does not become activated, and even though they accept a Great Vehicle system of tenets (Mind-Only School or Middle Way School), they follow the path of a hearer or solitary realizer for the time being. Being followers of, for instance, the Middle Way School by tenet, they must recognize that the third type of compassion is superior, but they do not see the possibility of making an effort at it now.

It would be unfortunate if, on top of this, such a person were to encounter a teacher who only encouraged him or her just to take care of him- or herself, especially if he or she is a person who, despite feeling that such great compassion is beyond him or her right now, is in fact capable of beginning to practice the Great Vehicle. It would be a great disservice to steer this person to a lower path, since the lower path would act as an obstacle by greatly lengthening the time it would take to reach highest enlightenment.

Also, if someone encourages a person capable of practicing the Great Vehicle to turn to the Lesser Vehicle path, this creates an obstacle to his own progress. Thus, it is important to emphasize that it is understandable for the third aspect of compassion to seem wildly beyond us. This is not a sign that we do not have the Great Vehicle lineage. If you simply like the notion of such compassion and begin work on the obstacles to it, your mind will begin flowing in that direction. Although you do not yet have a Great Vehicle path, you are activating the Great Vehicle lineage.

It is possible to fall from practice of the Great Vehicle despite having the Great Vehicle lineage. External circumstances are an important factor. If, for example, you are born in a place where Great Vehicle Buddhism is not present, you would not be able to meet with teachers who emphasize the aspect of compassion that takes the burden of others' suffering on oneself. As a young child in America, you might feel that is is wrong to kill bugs or throw stones at ducks or dogs, but other children might encourage you to do these things and call you "sissy" when you resisted. Eventually, you might join them. On top of this, you might encounter many adults—people you admired, such as your parents and their friends—who emphasized the importance of taking care of yourself by telling you to take care of "number one." Such things influence a person away from the bodhisattva path, but then when you hear about it, it again strikes your fancy. You begin undoing some of the obstacles you acquired earlier. Perhaps this is a sign that you made an effort to develop the Great Vehicle path in a previous life.

Difficult circumstances need not preclude development of great compassion. Buddha is said to have first generated it in one of the hells. He and another hell being were pulling a chariot of burning iron. Buddha felt compassion for his co-worker and, taking his rope, began to pull the whole load himself. A guardian of the hell observed this and began to beat Buddha, but Buddha persisted. This was his initial generation of the altruistic mind of enlightenment.

How did Buddha—how does anyone—get to the point of caring more for others' suffering than his own? We all know that it is very difficult to think, in the midst of a bad illness, for example, "May my sickness serve as the sickness of all beings, and may they thereby be spared from having to undergo it." One can develop such a thought by cultivating the switching of self and other. This is the Buddhist version of the golden rule; it is an instruction to cherish your neighbor as you used to cherish yourself, and to neglect yourself as you used to neglect others. Indeed, Buddhism teaches that the best way to take care of yourself is to care for others. It would be better for your motivation to be totally altruistic, of course, but the effect is there.

The Mind-Only School and Middle Way School teach that you become a bodhisattva, or actual Great Vehicle being, by path when you generate the altruistic intention to become enlightened for the sake of others. The mark of such generation is when this aspiration arises spontaneously outside of meditation just as strongly as it does during meditation. Your love and compassion have induced a deep and ever-present wish to transform yourself into a buddha so that you will be in a position to help others effectively. Right now, the help we can offer beings is very slight. Beyond that, it is difficult to tell whether we give more harm than help, even with the best intentions. Therefore those who are beings of the Great Vehicle by path want to purify themselves, not for the sake of being unusual, but in order to help others.

What is the mark of having the path of the Lesser Vehicle? Generation of the strong spontaneous wish, both in and out of meditation, to escape from cyclic existence. One sees life as a whirlwind of suffering. Even pleasure is seen as suffering, for pleasurable situations inevitably change; even neutral feeling is a form of suffering because one is caught in a process of contaminated conditioning.

Bodhisattvas also perceive things this way, because one must know one's own suffering before one can recognize that of others. The difference is that bodhisattvas immediately relate their understanding of suffering and their wish to leave cyclic existence to other beings. Thereby they generate great love and great compassion, which in turn induce the wish to attain buddhahood, a state not merely free from suffering but in which you have a perfection of mind and body that make you truly effective in helping others overcome their suffering.

Great compassion itself does not mean one has the path of the Great Vehicle, for compassion does not have buddhahood as its object. The object of observation of compassion is sentient beings, and its three subjective aspects, as mentioned earlier, are: (1) How nice it would be if all sentient beings were free from suffering and the causes of suffering, (2) May they be so freed, and (3) I myself will free them. This final aspect induces bodhichitta, an altruistic intention to become enlightened, which has two objects: the buddhahood one seeks to attain and the welfare of the beings for whose sake one will attain it. Buddhahood is seen as the means to achieve one's basic aim, the welfare of others. Although great compassion is closely related to this aspiration in that it induces the intention to become enlightened, they are not the same thing.

Thus, it is the altruistic intention to become enlightened that, when generated, is the mark of becoming a bodhisattva, of having entered the Great Vehicle path. Previous to that, you are engaged in the *practice* of the Great Vehicle path but have not yet generated it in your mental continuum. Therefore, the fact that you have not yet attained the altruistic aspiration does not mean you are a follower of the Lesser Vehicle. You are practicing the Great Vehicle in the sense that you are practicing becoming a being of the Great Vehicle.

9. THE TWO VEHICLES

Can you attain buddhahood through practicing the bodhisattva path as it is explained by one of the lower tenet systems—the Great Exposition School, the Sūtra School, the Mind-Only School, or the Middle Way Autonomy School? According to Dzong-ka-ba's exposition of the final system, the Middle Way Consequence School, it is not possible. It is not as if buddhahood were situated at a crossroads with each of the four tenet systems leading directly to it. Only one path leads to it—that of the Consequence School—but the other systems feed into it.

For that reason, even though there is only one final path, the other paths are not wrong. By enhancing your capacity through practicing them you become able to practice the final system. This viewpoint is quite different from contemporary claims that all paths are one. Nevertheless, they are one in the sense that, as long as it is appropriate to your capacity, a non-final path will be your true path in the sense of being helpful toward reaching the final goal. All spiritual paths are helpful for people who are appropriate vessels of that teaching, whether Buddhist or not.

The word "vehicle" has two meanings, and the distinction between the Lesser Vehicle and Great Vehicle must be made on the basis of one or both of these. Vehicle can be the *means* by which one progresses on the path, and it can also have the more unusual meaning of the *fruit* or *goal* toward which one progresses. In what sense is the latter a vehicle? We have said that a vehicle has the feature of being able to bear something. As a practice, it can bear you to a higher state; as a fruit or result of practice, it can bear your own or others' welfare. The fruit of foe destroyerhood bears your own welfare; the fruit of buddhahood, that of all sentient beings as well.

Since "vehicle" has these two meanings of means and of result, in examining the distinction between the Lesser and Great Vehicles we will find that they differ either in their types of practice, or in their goals, or in both.

There is a difference between the two vehicles in terms of the goal to which one progresses. One achieves different effects through practicing them. A practitioner of the Lesser Vehicle attains the fruit of foe destroyer; a practitioner of the Great Vehicle attains buddhahood. In what ways do these states differ? Both are thoroughly and forever liberated from cyclic existence, and thus both are forever freed from the afflictive emotions and will never again be subject to desire, hatred, or afflictive ignorance. However, buddhas have overcome the obstructions to omniscience whereas foe destroyers have not. Therefore, although a foe destroyer does not have any afflictive ignorance, he or she does have non-afflictive ignorance. Though afflictive ignorance and the afflictive emotions that it induces are difficult to abandon, foe destroyers are free of it. Being free from the ignorance that can induce afflictive emotions, they have no enmity, jealousy, anger, or miserliness, and so forth. However, buddhas have the additional special feature of being able to realize all objects of knowledge simultaneously. This means they know all objects and their emptinesses directly all of the time. A buddha has a very subtle knowledge of cause and effect that allows him or her to help others effectively. To understand how this relates to the meaning of vehicle as that able to bear something, let us look further into the obstructions that must be abandoned.

Obstructions to Liberation and Omniscience
The afflictive obstructions—preventers of liberation—are consciousnesses that conceive inherent existence and the afflictive emotions induced by it. We are drawn into desire, hatred, enmity, and so forth on the basis of our conception of objects as solid and concrete. The obstructions to omniscience are essentially the *appearances* of inherent

existence as well as the predispositions that cause these false appearances in phenomena. The conception of inherent existence is the activity of the subject, whereas the appearance of inherent existence *seems* to originate from the object, although it is actually due to a fault in the perceiving subject. For example, imagine that a magician can cause a small stone to appear as a delicious chocolate cake by reciting a mantra that affects the eye consciousness of everyone in the room, including himself. The audience does not know that he has cast a spell; they believe they are seeing an actual cake and begin to weave thoughts around it, "Perhaps I can arrange to get a piece after the show," or "Maybe he will start to pass it around soon." In other words, having made a mistake as to the nature of what is appearing, the audience is drawn into *useless* mental activity.

It is different for the magician. The stone does look like a cake to him, but he does not believe it. He is like a foe destroyer, for whom things still appear to have a concrete mode of existence but who will never assent to this appearance. Foe destroyers know through and through that the appearance of inherent, solid existence is false.

Sometimes in dreams you may realize that you are dreaming and thereafter as long as you keep remembering that you are dreaming, nothing can bother you even though the very fact of being mindful may cause the dream to become all the more intense. If something begins to bother you, you are able to hold deeply and tightly in mind that this is a dream. Then, when that consciousness weakens, you start believing in the dream once again. With the audience and magician, the appearance is the same in both cases, but the factor of belief is different. Foe destroyers are still subject to the appearance of inherent existence, but because they know fully that it is false, they are not drawn by it into afflictive emotions.

The appearance of inherent existence is the chief obstruction to omniscience. The inability to realize directly the emptiness of inherent existence while viewing objects is part and parcel of this false appearance. Only buddhas, who have overcome the obstructions to omniscience, can simultaneously and directly cognize both. Therefore, although foe destroyers are thoroughly familiar with emptiness and never forget the absence of inherent existence, they cannot always perceive emptiness directly. To do so, they must withdraw their sense consciousness from visible forms (colors and shapes), sounds, odors, tastes, tangible objects, and so forth. For as soon as their minds are involved in perceiving anything other than emptiness, they can no longer see emptiness directly. They may retain a deep state of mind and full implicit conceptual awareness of emptiness, but they do not cognize it directly as they move about in the world.

The inability to realize a phenomenon and its emptiness directly and simultaneously is an obstruction to omniscience; it goes hand in hand with the false sense perception of phenomena. This means that the *way* things appear prevents direct realization of emptiness. Similarly, direct realization of emptiness prevents cognition of other phenomena at that time. This is not because emptinesses and phenomena contradict each other but is due to our own incapacity in the form of the obstructions to omniscience.

These most subtle obstructions are extremely difficult to overcome, and it appears that most Indian religions do not take them into account. It may be that this is a distinctive feature of Buddhism. Indian religions usually speak of the necessity of coming out of trance in order to deal with other things. This is one reason why, according to Sāṃkhya, the liberated person must be alone. Nothing appears to such a being except pure consciousness. This is somewhat like the situation of a foe destroyer in meditative equipoise on emptiness.

Buddhas do not have to "come down" in any sense in order to participate in the world. They are simultaneously in and out of meditation. One cannot speak about "in and out of meditation" in a temporal sequence with respect to buddhas; they are always the same. This is unusual. Either it is a fantastic story concocted by the followers of the Great Vehicle, or it is a truly distinctive feature of Great Vehicle Buddhism.

The bodhisattva path is far longer than that of either the hearer or solitary realizer. The reason is that from the very beginning bodhisattvas aim to overcome the obstructions to omniscience, working to empower their mind, so that they can succeed at assisting others in the most effective way. Foe destroyers seek only to overcome the obstructions to liberation. Buddhas, having overcome both obstructions and attained omniscience, are able to secure not only their own welfare but that of countless sentient beings. Foe destroyers can be helpful to others, but because they lack subtle clairvoyance it is mostly a matter of guesswork. They do not have the certainty in action that buddhas, due to their extremely subtle clairvoyance, have. Compared to what buddhas can offer, foe destroyers' help is small.

Thus, the fruits of the two vehicles—foe destroyerhood and buddhahood—are different in terms of what they are able to bear or sustain, and once the vehicles in the sense of the goal to which one is progressing differ, the vehicles that are the means by which one is progressing will also differ. In other words, the paths, too, must differ. According to the Middle Way Consequence School, the Lesser Vehicle path is able to overcome the obstructions to liberation; it can overcome all conceptions of inherent existence whatsoever, not just in terms of the "I" but with regard to one's mind, body, house, and so forth. The bodhisattva path, in addition, is able to overcome the obstructions to omniscience.

PRACTICE VEHICLES

We have said that the fruit vehicle is the goal to which you are progressing and the practice vehicle, the means by which you progress. With respect to the means, all Buddhist practice can be included in method and wisdom. Therefore, if Lesser Vehicle and Great Vehicle differ also in the sense of being vehicles by which one progresses, the difference must come in method, wisdom, or both. According to the Middle Way Consequence School, the same realization of emptiness is required of both the Lesser Vehicle and the Great Vehicle practitioner. Both must realize the absence of inherent existence of phenomena. This is because both must get out of cyclic existence, and the only way to do this is to cultivate successfully the wisdom realizing phenomena as empty of inherent existence. Why is this wisdom essential for liberation?

Cyclic existence is an uncontrolled process of birth, aging, sickness, and death repeated over and over again, which is induced by a consciousness that conceives inherent existence and the afflictive emotions induced by that conception. ("Conception" means "consciousness that conceives"; thus, a conception of inherent existence is a consciousness that conceives inherent existence. This can only be a mental consciousness, not a sense consciousness.) On the basis of this tenet, it is said that the absence of inherent existence must be cognized before liberation can be attained. Therefore, one cannot get out of cyclic existence merely by withdrawing. One needs an antidote to the misconception on which cyclic existence is based. A wisdom consciousness that realizes emptiness is the antidote.

It is not sufficient merely to generate another consciousness that replaces ignorance, for ignorance can always find a way back. The wisdom consciousness must be an actual antidote that overcomes ignorance through its contradictory mode of apprehension, such that once the antidote is of sufficient strength, it is impossible for ignorance to recur. This is significant. There is no question that one can attain temporary freedom from problems of cyclic existence, such as anxiety, by concentrating on the breath and so forth, but such liberation is temporary because the anxiety can return.

It is easy to be fooled and think you have overcome something forever, when in fact your attainment is only temporary. If you achieve one of the deeper concentrations, you become able to maintain it continuously, so that the grosser afflictive emotions do not become manifest. Thus, one can be badly deceived. Buddhist systems of meditation warn against it from beginning to end. For there are many who develop and retain a stability of mind such that, no matter how they scrutinize their own minds, they have no sense whatever of possessing grosser afflictive emotions. Subtle ones remain but are difficult to identify.

A non-manifest afflictive emotion is not like an unconscious one in the Freudian sense. In the latter case, the unconscious mind is actively affecting the conscious mind, and it is possible to notice its effects, whereas in deep meditative states it seems impossible that desire, hatred, or ignorance could ever again become manifest. No matter how thoroughly you investigate your own mind at that time, not the slightest trace of these appears unless you have trained to recognize the subtle conception of inherent existence. Still, it is a mistake to assume they will never arise again. It would be like believing that because you do not see a spoon or some other object before you now, you will never see one again.

It is necessary to achieve a wisdom consciousness that is an actual antidote to the afflictive emotions, contradictory in its mode of apprehension to the sense of inherent existence that serves as the basis of the afflictive emotions. Otherwise, no matter how non-manifest afflictive emotions become, they are liable to return. One must cultivate an antidote to the mistaken consciousness that habitually assents to the false appearance of things. Thus, according to the Middle Way Consequence School, both practitioners of the Lesser and the Great Vehicles cultivate the wisdom realizing the most subtle emptiness that acts as such an antidote. The Mind-Only School and the Middle Way Autonomy School claim that the emptiness that a practitioner of the Great Vehicle realizes is subtler than what is realized by a practitioner of the Lesser Vehicle, but the Middle Way Consequence School emphatically disagrees. They say that all the great foe destroyers of the past had this subtlest of wisdoms.

This is not to say that the minds of buddhas and foe destroyers are equal in all ways. Buddhas engage in many other practices and achieve special characteristics as a result. A buddha's wisdom consciousness differs from a foe destroyer's because a buddha can realize all phenomena at the same time. Nevertheless, from the viewpoint of the emptiness being realized, their wisdom is the same.

Thus, according to the Middle Way Consequence School, there is no difference in wisdom between the two vehicles. Also, in cultivating this wisdom, both must attain a level of concentration of mind so that the consciousness that realizes emptiness will be sufficiently sharp and strong to act as an antidote. The mere understanding of emptiness does not serve as an antidote to the afflictive emotions. One must attain at least the concentrative level of calm abiding and team this with realization of emptiness. Then, one has to meditate over and over again. It is like washing something extremely dirty: First the grosser dirt washes out, but there is still the subtler dirt to be dealt with. Similarly, you have to soak the mind over and over again with the correct view of emptiness until it is thoroughly imbued with it, and the opposite conception is removed.

Since both the Lesser and Great Vehicles have this same realization of emptiness, the difference between the two vehicles cannot lie in wisdom and thus must lie in method. The special method of the Great Vehicle is the altruistic intention to become enlightened and the bodhisattva deeds it induces. The extraordinary feature of this aspiration is that one is intent on others' welfare and seeks buddhahood for their sake. This quality is the distinctive, precious feature of the Great Vehicle, praised above all else, because in dependence on it, one becomes a buddha. Without it, one attains, at most, the fruit of foe destroyerhood.

The attainment of buddhahood is prized for its capacity to help others. Foe destroyers cannot help on such a grand scale. They can cause a few people to become liberated from cyclic existence, but not to attain buddhahood. Buddhas can lead countless beings to highest perfect enlightenment.

As a result of their special love, compassion, and altruistic inspiration, bodhisattvas engage in the six perfections—giving, ethics, patience, effort, concentration, and wisdom. For example, bodhisattvas engage in giving in "limitless" ways over a "limitless" period of time in order to empower their wisdom consciousness so that it can overcome the obstructions to omniscience. An understanding of emptiness helps practice of the perfections. To take an extreme example, through thoroughly realizing that the body does not inherently exist, bodhisattvas become able to give even their bodies to hungry animals. There are many stories of Buddha's having done this during previous births. Bodhisattvas engage in limitless forms of merit for the sake of empowering their minds so that they can attain the station of becoming a limitless source of help and happiness. This is their motivation.

Because the enhancement of the wisdom consciousness to the point where it can overcome the obstructions to omniscience requires a great deal of virtuous mental power, it takes three periods of "countless" eons to complete the bodhisattva path. It takes that long for virtuous activities to empower the wisdom consciousness sufficiently. The virtues of giving and so forth alone—without wisdom—can never overcome either the conception or the appearance of inherent existence. Shāntideva says in his *Engaging in the Bodhisattva Deeds* (*byang chub sems dpa'i spyod pa la 'jug pa, bodhicaryāvatāra*, chap. 9, stanza 1) that all the branches of virtuous activity—worship, offering, and the other five perfections—are for the sake of wisdom, that is, for the sake of empowering the wisdom consciousness so that it can overcome these more subtle obstructions.

The importance of overcoming the obstructions to omniscience lies in the consequent ability to be of full service to others. Thus, even if altruism serves to enhance wisdom, that very wisdom is for the sake of effective altruism. In this way compassion is important in the beginning, middle, and end. Seeing this, practitioners aspiring to the Great Vehicle initially work hard at developing it to the point where it induces the intention to become enlightened for the sake of others. When training proceeds to the point where this intention is spontaneous, you become a bodhisattva, simultaneously attaining the first level of the Great Vehicle path, called the path of accumulation.

You have attained a spontaneous aspiration to enlightenment. It is as strong out of meditation as during it, but this does not mean it is active at all times, for if it were, you would never be able to think of anything else. However, it is always *ready* to become manifest, much as in our present state certain afflictive emotions are always ready to manifest. We only need someone to shout a certain way or treat us badly in some fashion, and hatred, enmity, and so forth are right there. A bodhisattva has only to see a hint of suffering to generate immediately a full-fledged intention to achieve buddhahood in order to eliminate quickly all such pain.

10. ENHANCEMENT OF WISDOM

The Lesser Vehicle tenet systems (the Great Exposition and Sūtra Schools) teach that in every age there is only one being who can successfully practice the bodhisattva path and attain buddhahood. In our age that person was Shākyamuni, and the next such special being will be Maitreya, much later. That is why, the Lesser Vehicle tenet systems say, Buddha did not teach people to follow his own path but taught paths suited to their own capacities, namely, the hearer and solitary realizer practices. Nevertheless, Buddha did relate stories about his own path and previous births as a bodhisattva, and followers of Lesser Vehicle tenet systems accept these literally. Therefore, they definitely do assert the existence of a bodhisattva path, but they do not look on it as something to adopt in their own practice.

Followers of the Lesser Vehicle tenet systems—the Great Exposition School and the Sūtra School—recognize that by practicing the paths of the Lesser Vehicle they will not achieve the type of physical body and mental clairvoyance that Buddha attained, but they hold that their thorough abandonment of afflictive obstructions will be the same as his. Beyond this, they say that they will in fact be fully equal to Buddha when they die, because, since all enlightened beings no longer need to take rebirth, they all disappear at death—foe destroyers and buddhas both. According to followers of Great Vehicle schools of tenets, this latter tenet is particularly inappropriate, for it indicates that the whole process of appearance is severed and that after the *parinirvāṇa*, or death, a buddha no longer has the ability to appear in the world. The reason for this Lesser Vehicle assertion is their conviction that cleansing the mind of afflictive emotions necessarily involves the eventual destruction of the mind at death. There is no possibility of pure appearance, for they see appearance as impelled by afflictive emotions.

How then do they explain the part of foe destroyers' lives subsequent to attainment of nirvāṇa? Foe destroyers do not disappear as soon as they become enlightened. Their life continues on the impetus of the contaminated action that caused them to take that particular rebirth. Until this is exhausted, they will not die. For even though their mind is purified such that no afflictive emotion can arise again, the force of the former afflictive emotions that impelled this last life still remains. However, their experience of the world after liberation is completely different from ours. It is like becoming aware that one is dreaming, but the dream continues. After the confusion of becoming involved with the beautiful or ugly dream appearances, frantically trying to find the classroom where the astronomy test is being given, for example, you understand that it is a dream and, though the images remain, you are no longer drawn into them. Similarly, a foe destroyer has no subjective need for, or attached involvement with, worldly appearances, but the force that set them up remains active.

Nirvāṇa With and Without Remainder

According to the Lesser Vehicle tenet systems, a nirvāṇa without remainder occurs when foe destroyers die. Their continuum of mind and body is severed—none of the physical or mental aggregates remain. This accords with the theory that in order to cleanse appearances you must make them vanish. A version of this idea is prevalent in Hinduism also. According to Sāṃkhya, just pure consciousness remains at the time of liberation. In Jainism, a non-physical body that is one-third the size of the liberated person's body floats to the top of the universe. There are no other appearances. According to the Lesser Vehicle schools, the whole process of appearance is annihilated.

The question of whether the process of appearance can be purified is crucial. The Middle Way Consequence School posits that the obstructions to omniscience are what prevent simultaneous direct realization of emptiness—the final reality—and conventional appearances. By overcoming these obstructions, one can retain the deepest realization of the status or mode of being of objects—their emptiness of inherent existence—while still allowing them to appear. This is the union of appearance and emptiness, one of the most profound and subtle topics of the Middle Way School.

Every Buddhist system of tenets except the Consequence School accepts that a nirvāṇa without remainder is the severance and disappearance of at least the mental and physical aggregates that are impelled by earlier contaminated actions and afflictive emotions. The nirvāṇa with remainder precedes this and is attained when all the obstructions to liberation are overcome, but the mind and body impelled by earlier contaminated actions and afflictive emotions still remain.

The Consequence School, in contrast, maintains that the nirvāṇa without remainder is attained first. In meditative equipoise, after much intense effort you finally overcome the last of the subtle obstructions to liberation. Your direct realization of emptiness has finally permeated the mind sufficiently to banish all the afflictive obstructions, resulting in attaining liberation from cyclic existence. This is the nirvāṇa without remainder. It is "remainderless" because at that time you not only have no lingering conception of inherent existence and thus have eradicated any possibility of assenting to seemingly inherent existence, but also have no false *appearance* of inherent existence in that you are directly realizing emptiness. Nothing else appears to your mind except emptiness. When you rise from meditative equipoise on emptiness—whether still in meditation but on other topics or whether risen from meditation altogether—your consciousness begins to pay attention to something other than emptiness. At this time the appearance of inherent existence remains; according to the Consequence School this is the time of a nirvāṇa with remainder. The person is beyond the afflictive emotions and thus has a nirvāṇa—the emptiness of the mind in the continuum of someone who has overcome all afflictive emotions—but is still beset by a remainder of the appearance of objects as if inherently existent.

According to the Great Vehicle schools of tenets, and specifically the Middle Way Consequence School, it is impossible for the continuum of mind and body to be completely severed. Even during deep trance when a long time can pass without your being aware of it and when you might think that the mental continuum had temporarily ceased, a subtle type of consciousness continues. The Consequence School emphatically denies the Lesser Vehicle contention that a foe destroyer's continuum ceases at death. In that case, they ask, who is it that attains the nirvāṇa without remainder as the Lesser Vehicle schools understand it? The Lesser Vehicle schools' answer is that the person who is *about to die* attains it, but this is difficult to uphold, for at the time of the remainderless nirvāṇa the person would have ceased.

All Great Vehicle schools except for the Mind-Only School following Asaṅga assert that, even for a foe destroyer, liberation from cyclic existence will not remain the final accomplishment. Eventually, buddhas rouse foe destroyers from the trance state that they enter after death and exhort them to enter the bodhisattva path. At that time foe destroyers again take rebirth, not by way of previous contaminated actions, but due to their own wish and the power of meditative stabilization.

The Mīmāṃsakas (according to Buddhist depictions)[30] believe that to cleanse the mind thoroughly is to destroy it. Even the Lesser Vehicle version of a nirvāṇa without remainder would be impossible, they say, because afflictive emotions dwell in the very entity of the mind. Freud and most psychologists would agree that we must learn to live with our problems because it is impossible to overcome them at their source. Indeed, our own self-image is so closely tied to certain afflictive emotions that it would be like carving out our own heart to imagine ourselves without them.

European and American scholars often say that the term nirvāṇa means to "blow out," but I have not seen this in any Buddhist text. Scholars upholding this etymology base it on the Sanskrit *nir* as "out" and *vāṇa* as coming from *vā* meaning "to blow." They then tie this down to the scriptural image of a butter lamp and say that blowing it out is a metaphor for nirvāṇa. The image that I have seen portrayed, however, is of the lamp's fuel—the butter or wax—being consumed; due to the consumption of the fuel, the flame is extinguished. The metaphor is not of blowing out a flame.

Tibetan translations of Sanskrit, which are famous for their literal accuracy either to the etymology, or the meaning, or an exposition based on a creative etymology, took the *vā* of nirvāṇa to be from the root *vṛt,* which means "to pass beyond." Thus the word nirvāṇa comes into Tibetan as "passed beyond sorrow" (mya ngan las 'das pa). Sorrow here is identified as the afflictive emotions; if you have an actual nirvāṇa, you have passed beyond all afflictive emotions utterly and forever.

In the Lesser Vehicle tenet systems (the Great Exposition and Sūtra Schools) this point comes when you attain a nirvāṇa with remainder. The mind and body, which get their impetus from former contaminated actions, remain, but there is no new generation of causes for being reborn in cyclic existence. Previous actions implanted the mind with a certain amount of power, and the foe destroyer continues to live as long as that power remains. Interruptions can cut this time short, but you cannot live beyond this allotment. In the Great Vehicle tenet systems, the obstructions to be overcome are not only those that keep you in cyclic existence but those that prevent attainment of the special omniscience and other qualities of buddhahood. To attain the nirvāṇa of a buddha—highest perfect enlightenment—it is necessary to overcome not only the *conception* of inherent existence that obstructs liberation but even the *appearance* of inherent existence, the chief obstruction to omniscience.

Lesser Vehicle and Great Vehicle Paths to Nirvāṇa

Each of the four schools of tenets describes the three vehicles—Hearer, Solitary Realizer, and Bodhisattva. Just as the Lesser Vehicle tenet systems set forth the bodhisattva path but do not emphasize it as something to practice, so the Great Vehicle schools relate the teachings of the solitary realizer and hearer paths but do not praise them as practices to be adopted. All schools recognize the tremendous difference in the motivation of practitioners of the two vehicles, bodhisattvas being more altruistic.

It is a rare and, in some ways, strange thing to take upon oneself the burden of joining each and every sentient being to happiness. This attitude, which is induced by love and compassion and is more precious than a wish-granting jewel, empowers the wisdom consciousness and thereby enables it to overcome the obstructions to omniscience. There are many internal resistances to cultivating such an attitude. For example, when you first generate a thought such as "I will liberate everyone in this city," pride arises such that you immediately feel, "It would be insufferable to have a thought like that," either because you would feel too prideful or because it simply seems crazy, like a charlatan who believes he can cure all illnesses by dabbing a bit of holy water here and there. This thought might cause you to set aside cultivation of this altruistic aspiration. However, this altruistic attitude is based on an estimation of the potential development of mind and body that make such determination realistic; by no means is it based on an assessment of one's present powers.

The wish to attain buddhahood for the sake of others is an active thought, and the Lesser Vehicle schools specifically teach that it is not to be generated except in very unusual cases. They consider that such an aspiration would interfere with their progress, because when they cultivate the four immeasurables—love, compassion, joy, and equanimity—the final achievement is equanimity. This is seen to be a subtler attitude than the others, and the type of mind that possesses it, more beneficial. Perhaps it is felt that an overriding concern for others would obstruct equanimity.

In the Great Vehicle schools it is just the opposite. Equanimity is the first step. You cultivate a realization that all beings are equal in the sense that all want happiness and not suffering. Thereby you develop an evenness of mind toward them. Moreover, if everyone is switching relationships—from friend to enemy and back again—from one lifetime to the next, how can you decide one-pointedly that a particular person is to be desired and another hated? Thus there is an equality both from the side of the object—other beings—and from one's own side. Such thoughts, as was mentioned earlier, are cultivated to prepare the mind, as you would smooth a wall, so that the mural of love, compassion, and joy can be painted on it. If you did not smooth out the mind beforehand, it would be very difficult to generate love for enemies. In the Lesser Vehicle systems, however, it seems that the point of developing love and compassion is to open yourself to the perception of everyone as equal.

Although the Middle Way Consequence School does not teach that one's own nirvāṇa is the highest attainment, it recognizes that some people culminate a temporary line of practice by achieving it. The great foe destroyers of the past were such people. They followed Middle Way Consequence School tenets but had not yet succeeded in generating the altruistic intention to become enlightened. However, they had realized emptiness as it is taught by the Consequence School. This is not surprising if you see that in Lesser Vehicle sūtras the Buddha often describes emptiness and selflessness just as the Consequence School sets them forth. In fact, lower tenet systems that maintain that Lesser Vehicle practitioners cultivate realization of another type of emptiness have a difficult time interpreting those passages.

We do not hear about many solitary realizers from the past because they generally did not speak. They remained alone. There are many solitary yogis in India even today, ascetics who leave everything and walk about with little or no clothing. Mainly they do retreats. Many solitary realizers do not speak, and even when they teach, they do it through hand signs. Because speech draws one into so many problems, they give it up completely; as a result, they do not become famous teachers. Moreover, they are proud, although this is not an afflicted pride. They want to achieve enlightenment without depending on anyone else in their final lifetime. They are born in a situation where they remember enough of the teaching to put it together and complete the path. Despite these differences, the scriptures often do not make a distinction between hearers and solitary realizers because their paths are so similar. Therefore, in discussing differences between the two vehicles, hearers and solitary realizers are considered together as the Lesser Vehicle.

If you understood emptiness, or selflessness, as it is described in the Great Exposition School, would you understand it in accordance with the Middle Way Consequence School's description of it? If you understood the one conceptually, would you understand the other also? The Consequence School teaches both coarse and subtle selflessness of persons as well as a subtle selflessness of phenomena. Their descriptions of these differ from what is taught in the lower schools. All the other tenet systems, from the Great Exposition School through to and including the Autonomy School, posit the non-existence of a permanent, unitary, and independent person as the coarse selflessness of persons and the non-existence of a self-sufficient, substantially existent person as the subtle selflessness of persons. The Lesser Vehicle schools do not posit a selflessness of phenomena; the Great Vehicle schools do, but the latter differ on what it is. All Great Vehicle schools except the Consequence School maintain that a bodhisattva practitioner realizes the subtle selflessness of phenomena and that the hearers and solitary realizers do not; they consider the selflessness of phenomena to be more subtle and difficult to understand than the selflessness of persons.

In the Consequence School, the subtle selflessness of persons is the person's lack of inherent existence, and the selflessness of phenomena is the lack of inherent existence of phenomena other than the person. Thus, unlike the lower Great Vehicle systems, the Consequence School considers the selflessness of persons and phenomena to be equally subtle. In order to understand either one, it is necessary to realize the absence of inherent existence. This is the emptiness that any practitioner must realize and then cultivate in direct perception in order to be liberated from cyclic existence, for a consciousness that conceives inherent existence is the root cause of cyclic existence.

This means that, according to the Consequence School, the Lesser Vehicle schools do not even know how to present a path of liberation from cyclic existence, because the Lesser Vehicle tenet systems incorrectly describe how to become a foe destroyer. In this sense, the Consequence School is exclusive. In another sense, however, it is inclusive because it teaches that all the great foe destroyers of the past realized the same most subtle emptiness that the Consequence School describes. It is important to remember that, except for the Yogic Autonomy Middle Way School, all the non-Consequence School tenet systems assert that Lesser Vehicle practitioners *only* realize the subtle selflessness of persons.[31] Thus those that posit a selflessness of phenomena make a vast difference between the realization of the selflessness of persons and that of phenomena.

In Theravāda it is said that the person does not exist, that there is only mind and body. The person is seen to have a different status from that of mind and body. Still, despite their making statements that the person does not exist, their teaching as a whole flows in the direction of asserting that the collection of mind and body is the person. Thus the person does exist, although not in the coarse way we usually think it does. What is significant here is that the type of selflessness they ascribe to persons—the lack of a self-sufficiency or substantial existence—is not understood with respect to phenomena. This fact itself shows that they are not talking about the same selflessness that the Consequence School describes, because the lack of inherent existence applies *equally* to persons and other phenomena, whereas the lack of self-sufficiency is asserted to be a quality of persons only. Because of this difference, it can be determined that it is not merely the case that the Consequence School and other schools use different but synonymous terms for emptiness; the descriptions themselves are different.

It is unlikely that the Consequence School is talking about something so gross that, of course, it would apply equally to persons and other phenomena. For example, persons and other phenomena are equally "non-horns of a rabbit." True enough, but totally insignificant. No one conceives persons and other phenomena to be "the horns of a rabbit." Even if certain circumstances caused you to think at one time or another, "That rabbit has horns," such a mistake would not draw you into cyclic existence. Hence, it is also clear that the Middle Way Consequence School is not just talking about a philosophical principle that it fabricated and superimposed on phenomena and then offering an antidote to help us overcome that. Since they are not talking about such a coarse factor, their emptiness must, as described above, be subtler than what the other systems teach and, due to its subtlety, is suitable to be a quality of everything that exists.

What is the conception of a coarse self of persons—that is to say, as being substantially existent in the sense of being self-sufficient? You can catch a sense of it when you are very excited or proud, or when someone has given you something you really like, or taken away something of which you are very fond. At such times you feel as though you had your own separate entity, as though you were solid, something like a marble sitting in a piece of meat. At times of very strong feeling, such as when you are shaking with anger, the sense of "I" is so strong that it may even seem to be a separate entity from mind and body, something that you could just lift out from among the mental and physical aggregates. You may experience this as the controller of mind and body. For example, if someone compliments you on your hair or clothing, something inside lights up as if it were the owner of these praiseworthy things. Or when you are falsely accused and everyone is pointing their fingers at you, you have a palpable sense of an "I" that is not just the collection of mind and body. At other milder times, the "I" may seem to be just the collection of mind and body. All schools except the Consequence School find no fault with this last conception, but the Consequence School says that even this type of self—although subtler than that which is experienced as almost having a separate entity from mind and body—cannot be found under analysis and hence does not exist in the way in which we conceive it. Beyond all of these, there is a conventionally existent self, but it takes a great deal of thought and practice to understand what it is.

11. METHOD AND WISDOM

Both the Middle Way Consequence School and the Lesser Vehicle tenet systems (the Great Exposition and Sūtra Schools) assert that the practitioners of all three vehicles achieve the same type of wisdom realization, though they differ as to what that wisdom realization is. According to the Consequence School, since a consciousness that conceives inherent existence is the cause of cyclic existence, anyone who achieves liberation must overcome it. The Lesser Vehicle systems hold the same with respect to a consciousness that conceives a substantially existent person. According to the Mind-Only and Autonomy Schools, however, those who are definite in the bodhisattva lineage realize a more subtle emptiness than hearers or solitary realizers; they make effort—from the very beginning of their path—at this more profound realization and along the way overcome cyclic existence.

Wisdom is the sixth perfection, and the wisdom consciousness receives empowerment from the merit of performing the other perfections. Thus, there are the two collections—of merit and of wisdom. There are different ways of explaining these two collections in terms of the six perfections. It can be said that the collection of merit consists of the first three perfections—giving, ethics, and patience—and that the collection of wisdom is the last two—concentration and wisdom— with the fourth perfection, effort, being related to both collections. Another explanation is that the first five perfections are the collection of merit because the perfection of concentration is taken to refer to the worldly concentrations that do not take emptiness as their object. These concentrations merely increase mental stability and dexterity and thus would not be included within the collection of wisdom. For the sake of simplicity of expression, the effort aspect of wisdom is disregarded, and therefore only the sixth perfection is included in the wisdom collection.

It is also possible to take the first three perfections—giving, ethics, and patience—as the collection of merit, the next two—effort and concentration—as shared, because effort and concentration apply to both collections, and the sixth perfection itself is the collection of wisdom. Even though in general the collection of merit refers to the first three, it is implicit that these include the aspects of effort and concentration. In any case, the point is that activities such as engaging in limitless types of giving empower the wisdom consciousness so that it eventually can overcome the obstructions to omniscience. What is it about giving that empowers wisdom? It is not that one gains new knowledge through giving—the enhancement must be due to other factors. It is not explained how this happens; somehow the activity of charity on such a thorough and continual scale opens the mind to a greater level of power.

Foe destroyers achieve wisdom without practicing the perfections of giving, ethics, and patience, and thus they overcome only the obstructions to liberation. For bodhisattvas, the ability of the wisdom consciousness to overcome the obstructions to omniscience is a result of practicing the perfections of giving, ethics, and patience in "limitless" ways over a "limitless" period of time.

The attainment of the path of accumulation, which marks the beginning of a bodhisattva's first period of countless great eons of collecting merit, is simultaneous with initial generation of the mind of enlightenment—the altruistic intention to attain buddhahood. Most of that first period of countless great eons is spent on the path of accumulation.

It takes bodhisattvas at least two periods of countless great eons to overcome cyclic existence, even though they are said to be much brighter than the foe destroyer who can, at the quickest, attain liberation within three lifetimes. The wisdom that each attains is the same, but the amount of merit that empowers that wisdom is vastly different.

Both succeed similarly in that neither will ever again generate a consciousness that conceives inherent existence or the afflictive emotions that arise from it; both are equally liberated. Thus, you might think, why not first take the path of a hearer and overcome cyclic existence in three lifetimes? Once liberation has been achieved and your own suffering overcome, you could enter the bodhisattva path of accumulation and begin amassing merit so that you could attain buddhahood and establish the welfare of others. Otherwise, you might reason, you could fall from the bodhisattva path and have to start all over again.

To get at this issue using a different approach, the path of accumulation, the first of the five paths, has three parts: great, middling, and small. From the middling path of accumulation you are irreversible in the sense that the path to enlightenment will never be turned around—you will never fall from being a bodhisattva. Most bodhisattvas actually enter the path of accumulation at this level; thus, they are irreversible right from the beginning. However, only with the achievement of the eighth ground do you overcome the obstructions to liberation, something that the foe destroyer can overcome without even practicing for one eon, never mind two periods of countless great eons. Why then is it not recommended that you complete the hearer path before entering that of the bodhisattva?

One answer is that you cannot assume that, having attained the fruit of a foe destroyer, it will then take you only three periods of countless great eons to reach buddhahood. It is true that you would already have overcome the afflictive obstructions; you would not have to work newly to realize emptiness directly, for you would have already done that. However, you would have wasted all the time it took you to reach foe destroyerhood in the sense that you could have used that time to accumulate the merit that empowers the wisdom consciousness. Not only that, but in practicing the hearer path, the mind becomes addicted to following one's own purpose rather than that of others, and this creates tremendous obstacles even to entering the bodhisattva path as well as to practicing it once you have entered it. Far from completing the path in three periods of countless great eons, it might take six, twelve, or forty-three periods of countless great eons.

The whole process has thus been lengthened greatly; it is not just a matter of extending it by three lifetimes.

Once you have understood emptiness—and this does not mean to realize it directly, but simply to understand it—and, in addition to this, have generated the altruistic aspiration to enlightenment and thereby entered the bodhisattva path, you are irreversible as a bodhisattva, being on the middling path of accumulation. This means you will never fall from your great compassion, love, and the altruistic intention induced by these. This is called a gold-like intention to become enlightened.

Still, the generation of the bodhisattva attitude does not preclude also having Lesser Vehicle vows, for the bodhisattva vow can be taken by monastics (that is, nuns and monks) and householders, and monastics' and householders' vows themselves are Lesser Vehicle. Thus, the same person who holds a bodhisattva vow could also have Lesser Vehicle vows and could also have tantric vows, which are still harder than the others.

To have an altruistic intention to become enlightened means that you have considered people individually for a long time in all the different types of cyclic existence—all the many varieties of hell beings, hungry ghosts, animals, humans, demigods, and gods. It is necessary to reflect on these individually over and over. When we *talk* about developing the altruistic intention, we describe one type of thought and then move on to the next. However, when you actually cultivate it, you must remain with one contemplation for a long time—for example, reflecting on the suffering of one type of person, then another, then the next and the next, and so on. Similarly, you methodically reflect on your closeness to each of these beings with the recognition that all have been friends and relatives in innumerable former lifetimes. It is only due to our present craziness that we do not know each other and that we seem to have eternal enemies or to be unconnected with people around us.

One works at generating the three aspects of compassion with respect to sentient beings individually. To reflect singly on every person you have known in this lifetime, thinking, "May this person be free of suffering and the causes of suffering," would take a while, but not too long—perhaps ten days, two weeks, or at the most a month. But to generate a spontaneous feeling with regard to all sentient beings takes much longer. Yet, in this way one can work through the three aspects through to, and including, the unusually altruistic attitude: "I will cause all beings to be free of suffering and the causes of suffering, even if I have to do it alone."

At this point you must take stock of your actual situation. "Can I succeed in freeing beings from suffering? What type of person would I have to be in order to be able to accomplish such altruistic wishes?" You can easily conclude that you do not now have the ability to free beings from suffering and establish them in happiness. You can recognize that only buddhas are capable of such; therefore, you must investigate whether or not it is possible to attain buddhahood. Is it just a myth or is it something that can actually be achieved? At this point, sharp people research the nature of the mind. They understand with valid cognition that it is empty of inherent existence and that consequently the attainment of enlightenment is possible. Seeing this, they make a strong promise to attain buddhahood for the sake of others.

The full-fledged spontaneous wish to attain buddhahood in order to achieve others' welfare has two objects: the welfare of the beings to be helped, your object of intent, and buddhahood itself, the object of attainment. At this point, whether you have previously attained foe destroyerhood or not, you initially enter the bodhisattva path of accumulation. Preferably, you would enter the Great Vehicle from the beginning, without going through the Lesser Vehicle path. For no matter how marvelous that path seems, from the bodhisattva perspective it is considered a tremendous waste of time. The mind becomes addicted to self-cherishing during a time of intense concentration, making it such that although foe destroyers have abandoned afflicted self-cherishing, they still have a non-afflicted self-cherishing.

What it boils down to is the question of which goal is realistic. Is there really such a thing as buddhahood, or is it imaginary, like a cloak made of turtle hairs? Can the altruistic aspiration be realized? If it can, then followers of the Great Vehicle have a program to offer those whose sensibilities are suited for it. They do not claim that theirs is the path for everyone to follow now, although they do say that everyone will eventually achieve buddhahood through it.

The Lesser Vehicle schools teach that once foe destroyers die, they disappear. There is no question that until their death they will act with strong compassion to help others. They definitely have the first two aspects of compassion. But the Lesser Vehicle schools feel that the Great Vehicle schools are wrong about the possibility of accomplishing the welfare of all beings, because there is not enough time in the remainder of a single life. Once the mind has been thoroughly cleansed and the life spent, it will cease; thus there is no possibility of continuing to work for others. Proponents of the Lesser and Great Vehicle tenet systems disagree most significantly on this point.

Whether the final nirvāṇa is the end, as the Lesser Vehicle schools say, or a new type of beginning, as most of the Great Vehicle schools maintain, depends to a large extent on whether or not it is possible to generate a body of pure thought. Our ordinary bodies are generated by contaminated actions; when these are exhausted, is there or is there not a means by which we can manifest in the world and engage in helpful activity? This is a difficult matter on which to gain conviction. It probably would not be necessary to achieve such a capacity yourself before believing in it; perhaps seeing someone else succeed at it would be convincing; perhaps contemplating your own mind would assuage some doubt. In any case, it is clear that the direction of the Lesser Vehicle path, as explained in the Lesser Vehicle schools, is toward achievement of a neutral state. Practitioners do not seek anything beyond that, and their main direction of mind is absorbed in it. If their goal is realistic and the other is not, they are at an advantage. This is because the direction of the path as described in the Great Vehicle schools, as revealed over and over again in the structure of its path, is to bring the practitioner to a deep state of realization *and then out again in altruistic activity*. In the end, that deep mind of realization is used as the substance of active appearance, whereby the deep realization and compassionate appearance can occur simultaneously.

Everything in the practice vehicle is included within method and wisdom. Moreover, from the perspective of the Great Vehicle schools, practice of the Lesser Vehicle is a branch of the process of achieving highest enlightenment for those whose capacities are suited to it. The thought to get out of cyclic existence that, when it arises spontaneously night and day, marks the beginning of the Lesser Vehicle path of accumulation is also cultivated in the Great Vehicle path. One has succeeded at it when one never—even for a moment—comes to admire the prosperity of cyclic existence. Desirous or hateful thoughts might still arise but, as Khetsun Sangpo (see *Tantric Practice in Nying-ma*, p. 61) has said, you just let them disappear. You are so strongly convinced that the nature of worldly life is suffering that nothing tempts you or elicits admiration. The thought to get out of cyclic existence is the first principal aspect of the path and part of the impetus for practice of either vehicle.

Buddha's teaching bears the imprint of four seals, so called because just as you might seal a letter with hot wax stamped with your insignia to mark it as yours, so all Buddhist schools teach systems sealed with these, marking these teachings as Buddha's:

1. All products are impermanent.
2. All contaminated things are miserable.
3. All phenomena are selfless.
4. Nirvāṇa is peace.

These are not to be accepted on blind faith; they are not unconscious assumptions but tenets based on reason, which, in turn, is based on observation.

The Lesser Vehicle schools say that the Great Vehicle schools contradict the first seal's teaching that all products are impermanent. If such is the case, they ask, how can a buddha's complete enjoyment body be immortal as the followers of the Great Vehicle claim? For the Great Vehicle, there is no contradiction, however. Since an enjoyment body arises in dependence on its cause—the Great Vehicle path—it is impermanent, but its type does not change moment by moment as do our own minds and bodies, and from this viewpoint it can be *called* permanent even though it is impermanent. A buddha's complete enjoyment body does not age or become wrinkled. Thus it is immortal; its continuum is everlasting.

The Lesser Vehicle schools also object to the Great Vehicle teaching because they believe it contradicts the second seal's assertion that all contaminated things are miserable. According to the Lesser Vehicle tenet systems, even the body of a foe destroyer is contaminated, whereas the Great Vehicle describes many types of joy and bliss along the path. For example, the first bodhisattva ground is called "the joyous." However, the Great Vehicle tenet systems answer that the main fact about the first bodhisattva ground is that it is a direct realization of emptiness, and even the Lesser Vehicle schools would have to agree that a mind non-dually realizing emptiness is not contaminated because it is not suitable to increase contamination. On the contrary, such a mind is an antidote to the contaminating afflictive emotions. Also, joy is not necessarily afflictive.

Great Vehicle systems refer to buddhas and bodhisattvas as *mahātma,* which translates as "great self." The lower systems fault the higher for applying such a name to the foremost teacher of selflessness in seeming contradiction to the third seal that all phenomena are selfless. However, the Great Vehicle tenet systems answer that this name indicates not that buddhas and bodhisattvas have a self such as the view of selflessness negates, but simply that they are people endowed with a greatly altruistic attitude.

Proponents of Great Vehicle tenets maintain that even after achieving the nirvāṇa of a foe destroyer one must continue to make effort over periods of countless great eons in order to achieve buddhahood. This, say the Lesser Vehicle systems, contradicts the fourth seal, which teaches that nirvāṇa is peace. However, the Great Vehicle tenet systems answer that foe destroyers' nirvāṇa is peaceful in the sense that they attain a total cessation or pacification of the afflictive emotions obstructing liberation. This is not a temporary nirvāṇa because those afflictive emotions will never return; nevertheless, there is more to be done. In that case, a follower of a Lesser Vehicle school might reply, why did Buddha sometimes teach that there was nothing more to be done after attaining liberation? Why did he teach that the Lesser

Vehicle nirvāṇa is final? The Great Vehicle tenet systems answer that a sūtra tells how Buddha magically created an island so that some shipwrecked travelers could catch their breath before continuing on and, similarly, Buddha gives those not ready to enter the Great Vehicle a goal they can keep in sight; once they get there, they are ready to hear about the remainder of the path. Eventually they will overcome the obstructions to omniscience and thereby attain the capacity of simultaneous realization of all things.

Those who are Lesser Vehicle by tenet do not accept such a description of Buddha's wisdom. According to them, buddhahood is the complete destruction of all afflictive emotions that is accompanied by attainment of special, serial knowledge of all phenomena; buddhas can know anything they want to by turning their mind, point by point, to it. Buddhas' knowledge has no limits due to time or space, but they can only reflect on one thing at a time; they are all-knowing in the sense that they can know anything they wish by turning their mind to it, but not in the Great Vehicle sense of realizing everything simultaneously. Thus, according to the Great Vehicle schools, a "buddha" as described in the Lesser Vehicle schools still has a non-afflicted type of ignorance inasmuch as obstructions that prevent *simultaneous* knowledge of all things remain. There is a story of Shākyamuni Buddha's asking a local deity, "What is happening in your territory nowadays?" The Lesser Vehicle schools take this as a sign of Buddha's not wanting to think about something himself. According to the Great Vehicle schools, Buddha would have engaged in such conversation simply to be of help to the other being.

According to the Consequence School, the buddhahood described by Lesser Vehicle tenet systems is not buddhahood at all, for such a buddha is depicted as realizing a very coarse type of emptiness. Such a being has not even attained liberation from cyclic existence, for only realization of, and prolonged meditation on, the subtlest type of emptiness—the lack of inherent existence—overcomes the afflictive obstructions that prevent liberation. Such a being cannot directly realize phenomena and their emptiness at the same time, whereas a buddha, as described in the Great Vehicle, can.

12. QUINTESSENTIAL DISTINCTIONS BETWEEN THE LESSER AND GREAT VEHICLES

Before discussing the special feature of the Mantra Vehicle, it is appropriate to review the quintessential distinctions mentioned so far between the Lesser and the Great Vehicles.[32]

1. The Dalai Lama teaches that one needs to combine learnedness, practical application, and a good mind. Therefore, mere learning about the differences between the vehicles is not sufficient.

2. Generation of a good mind is the essential purpose of differentiating the vehicles. The immediate purpose is to know the difference between the vehicles in order to facilitate practice.

These set the tone. They indicate the manner in which the topic should be approached and the type of attitude that should be avoided. Even someone studying Buddhism academically with no intention to practice either vehicle should be aware that from the Buddhist point of view mere learnedness is not sufficient. He or she should take the time to build up a full imagination of how a Buddhist goes about this study.

It is marvelous to reflect that the complex structure that emerges in a detailed study of Buddhism is in fact all for the sake of a good mind. This means a relaxed mind, not one given to nervousness, tension, and so forth, but one conducive to love and compassion. It includes a low level goodness and does not necessarily mean that one has succeeded in generating love and compassion. It is not always easy to put more emphasis on a good mind than on learnedness. For example, one may attend a lecture and, without reflecting on the teacher's kindness in giving it, immediately criticize her or him for what one sees as faults.

Rather, our attitude should be like a bee that takes pollen from a flower and leaves without doing it any harm.

Still, learnedness is important. If you can combine it with practical application and a good mind, this is supreme. If, however, your capacity is such that a choice must be made between learnedness and practical application, the Dalai Lama advises in his "Key to the Middle Way"[33] that one emphasize the latter. Why? Learnedness alone can bring trouble—jealousy, competitiveness, and so forth—whereas a sense of practical application, which automatically involves a good mind, will always be beneficial.

The generation of a good mind, the fulfillment of which is the attainment of buddhahood, is the essential purpose of differentiating the vehicles. The immediate purpose is to know their distinguishing features for the sake of facilitating practice. Some people find it easier to make an effort at their own practice when they know how it fits into the path as a whole and how it leads to the higher practices.

3. One can distinguish the terms "Lesser Vehicle" and "Great Vehicle" from the viewpoint of schools of tenets and from the viewpoint of path.

One may be able to assume a Great Vehicle tenet system but unable to take up the bodhisattva path. One who attains even the Lesser Vehicle path of accumulation is never tempted for a moment by any of the marvels of cyclic existence and has an unwavering determination to leave it.

If you use knowledge of a Great Vehicle tenet system, such as the Mind-Only School or the Middle Way School, to dominate others, this, of course, contradicts the central purpose of learning it in the first place. Merely studying a system is by no means tantamount to practicing it. Moreover, without the proper motivation, study of the vehicles can lead to more difficulties, because the very means that have the potential for freeing you from cyclic existence are being used to lock you in.

4. One can be a follower of the Great Vehicle by tenet and a Lesser Vehicle practitioner by path, as in the case of the great foe destroyers of the past. Thus, there are some capable of assuming a Great Vehicle tenet system who are temporarily incapable of generating a Great Vehicle path.

5. The two Lesser Vehicle tenet systems (the Great Exposition and Sūtra Schools) and the two Great Vehicle tenet systems (the Mind-Only and Middle Way Schools) each present a Lesser Vehicle path (hearer and solitary realizer paths) and a Great Vehicle path (bodhisattva path).

6. The reason for the four schools of tenets is peoples' different capacities, including the pride of wanting the highest despite being incapable of it; thus, low, non-final systems are taught as if they were final.

The Consequence School, considered the highest system, has a complete presentation of the lower and higher reaches of the path. However, people need way stations, situations in which they do not have the distraction of even hearing about practices beyond their own.

7. The distinction between the Lesser and Great Vehicles and between the two Great Vehicles (Perfection Vehicle and Mantra Vehicle) must be found in the sense of vehicle as the goal toward which one progresses (the fruit) and/or as the means by which one progresses (method, wisdom, or both).

8. Valid foundation and the conditionable nature of the mind make limitless development of method and wisdom possible.

It is said that because method and wisdom are true and can be certified by valid cognition, cultivation of them will lead to buddhahood, the fruit vehicle. "Conditionable nature of the mind" means that if you practice continuously and effectively, it is not necessary to start back at the beginning every time you meditate. The mind's nature is such that something is left over from former practice. A rigorous proof of the mind's ultimate conditionability involves establishing phenomena as empty of inherent existence and ascertaining that one has been reborn in cyclic existence repeatedly since beginningless time. Then, once the mind is capable of being altered by practice and once there is a limitless amount of time in which to engage in practice, it is possible to develop limitless mental capacities. The mind can become fully omniscient and able to realize directly both phenomena and their emptinesses simultaneously.

9. *The distinction between the Lesser and Great Vehicles lies in the sense of vehicle as that toward which one is progressing (the states of foe destroyer and buddha, respectively, which bear, like a vehicle, the welfare of only oneself and of all sentient beings) and in the sense of vehicle as those practices by which one progresses (specifically method, not wisdom).*

10. *From the viewpoint of the Middle Way Consequence School, the wisdom of both vehicles is the same because the root of cyclic existence is a consciousness that conceives of persons and other phenomena as inherently existent. Hence, it must be overcome by all who seek liberation from cyclic existence, and Lesser Vehicle foe destroyers*[34] *(those who have attained the fruit of Lesser Vehicle paths) are indeed liberated from cyclic existence.*

11. *Therefore, both the Lesser and Great Vehicle paths involve realization of the subtle emptiness that is the lack of inherent existence of persons and other phenomena.*

The Consequence School teaches that through no other tenet system can you free yourself from cyclic existence. We have already discussed the fact that Buddha dispensed different systems like so many medicines to suit the needs of his trainees. It can be something of a shock to hear that the great systematizers of these teachings, masters like Vasumitra, Vasubandhu, Dharmakīrti, Shāntarakṣhita, Kamalashīla, Bhāvaviveka, and Jñānagarbha, did not set forth a path that would itself bestow even liberation, let alone omniscience. This perspective, however, is clear in the writings of the principal promulgator of the Consequence School, Chandrakīrti.[35]

The Ge-luk-ɓa order, which is Consequentialist in terms of its own final system, was founded by Dzong-ka-ɓa (1357–1419) and became the "dominant" system in Tibet—it had the most followers and the greatest political power.[36] The Ge-luk-ɓas present the tenets of the Consequence School in reliance upon Chandrakīrti's texts, as do all of the other major orders in Tibet. He is said to have been a tenth-ground bodhisattva who descended from high in the world system for the express purpose of setting straight Nāgārjuna's teaching. Dzong-ka-ɓa cogently shows that on several occasions Chandrakīrti clearly states that, even to attain the fruit of the Hearer or Solitary Realizer Vehicles, one must realize the most subtle emptiness.

Chandrakīrti's reason for asserting this is that the conception of persons and other phenomena as inherently existent is the root of cyclic existence. The lower tenet systems vigorously contest this. The Great Exposition, Sūtra, and Mind-Only Schools as well as the two divisions of the Autonomy School maintain with one voice that by realizing what the Consequence School considers a coarse emptiness it is indeed possible to attain liberation. They claim that a consciousness that conceives inherent existence is *not* the root of cyclic existence. This is a key point to settle. It is clear that the Consequence School and non-Consequentialist systems are describing different types of realizations; it is not just a matter of their referring to the same type of emptiness but of giving it different names.

The selflessness that the other systems say is necessary to realize in order to free oneself from cyclic existence is a quality that applies only to persons, whereas the Consequence School's subtle emptiness is equally a quality of persons and other phenomena. Thus, we can decide that the emptiness they strive to realize is different.

12. Therefore, the difference between the Lesser Vehicle and the Great Vehicle in the sense of vehicle as that by which one progresses lies not in wisdom but in method—motivation and its attendant deeds. The Lesser Vehicle motivation is the wish to attain liberation from cyclic existence for oneself, whereas the Great Vehicle motivation is the wish to attain buddhahood in order to help all sentient beings.

The bodhisattva's motivation and practice of the perfections of giving and so forth lend a power to the wisdom consciousness that the wisdom consciousness of a Lesser Vehicle practitioner does not have. Certainly such training would shape the personality, and something about its effect on the psyche enables the bodhisattva to overcome the obstructions to omniscience and achieve direct, simultaneous cognition of the two truths.

The fact that hearers or solitary realizers are motivated by a wish to attain their own liberation does not mean they are not compassionate.

But they do not have the extraordinary thought to take upon themselves the burden of freeing all sentient beings. Their compassion is appreciably greater than our own; yet, if we had awakened the Great Vehicle compassion, our compassion would be more significant than theirs. Although Lesser Vehicle practitioners' limitless compassion may be conjoined with one-pointed meditative equipoise that can remain unbroken for days, a few moments of Great Vehicle compassion is more valuable. Upholders of Lesser Vehicle tenet systems would not argue with the Consequence School's assertion that hearers and so forth do not generate great compassion; they feel it would be unreasonable to wish to separate all beings from suffering because they do not accept the possibility of taking rebirth by the power of prayer petitions and so forth once one has achieved nirvāṇa. For Lesser Vehicle practitioners, compassion is a secondary feature of the path, not the primary motivation.

> *13. There are two kinds of obstructions: afflictive obstructions (preventing liberation from cyclic existence) and obstructions to omniscience (preventing simultaneous cognition of the two truths—ultimate truths and conventional truths, or emptinesses and other objects qualified by emptiness).*

The chief obstruction to omniscience is the false appearance of phenomena as inherently existent. This prevents the mind from realizing the two truths directly and simultaneously. What one wants to attain is a view perceiving the interpenetration of appearance and emptiness, the union of appearance and emptiness.

> *14. The afflictive obstructions are (1) the ignorance that conceives the inherent existence of persons and other phenomena, (2) the other afflictive emotions that this induces, and (3) their seeds.*

Any potency of the mind that could produce an afflictive obstruction is overcome when the afflictive obstructions are overcome. Regarding this, a consciousness that conceives inherent existence produces many types of afflictive emotions—innate, artificial, coarse, and subtle. Most meditation systems train one to withdraw from afflictive thought, from problems. This is not sufficient. It is sometimes necessary temporarily to withdraw from certain problems in order to attain the strength of mind to overcome them, but no matter how fantastic a state one achieves by such methods, it is not sufficient. Such withdrawal is like going to a fancy restaurant when you get tired of your usual one. You are in a new place and an entirely different scene is generated, but the underlying propensity for boredom has not been removed. In meditation one can achieve tremendous worldly happiness—greater than one would find by relying on external factors—but it would be a mistake to confuse this bliss with actual liberation from worldliness. Certain blissful states are indeed conducive to liberation; calm abiding is, but it must be teamed with insight. Thus it is important to recognize worldly meditations for what they are; they can be useful on the spiritual path as long as one knows their place and does not view them as the final attainment.

15. *Obstructions to omniscience are predispositions that are established by a consciousness that conceives inherent existence but that produce the false appearance of inherent existence as well as the incapacity to realize the two truths directly and simultaneously.*

16. *If one's aim is merely to abandon the afflictive obstructions, it is sufficient to approach emptiness through just a few forms of reasoning. If one's aim is to eradicate the obstructions to omniscience and thereby attain buddhahood, it is necessary to approach emptiness through limitless forms of reasoning.*

Lesser Vehicle practitioners use only a few types of reasoning to gain understanding of emptiness, whereas Great Vehicle practitioners use many. This is how the practice of realizing emptiness differs between the two vehicles according to the Consequence School. Although Lesser Vehicle practitioners realize the same emptiness as those of the Great Vehicle, they are duller; they do not spread their minds out to encompass many ways of approaching emptiness. A bodhisattva welcomes the opportunity to reflect on emptiness from many different viewpoints.

For example, an action can be analyzed from the viewpoint of its object, or its agent, or the action itself. Any two of these could also be taken in combination. Similarly, you can analyze something from the viewpoint of (1) its having been made by its causes, (2) its producing effects, or (3) its own entity, analyzing whether any of these exist the way they appear. That thing could also be analyzed in the context of its being a basis that possesses various qualities.

One famous method for approaching emptiness is analyzing the "I" and its relation to mind and body. You begin by observing your sense of mind and body—whether the "I" is among these or separate from them. It is enough to crack your head open just to think about this.

Nāgārjuna's *Treatise on the Middle (dbu ma'i bstan bcos, madhyamakaśāstra)* contains twenty-seven chapters; the second of these alone has ten types of analysis approaching emptiness. It takes a year to read such a chapter carefully—with commentary by Chandrakīrti—not because the Sanskrit is difficult but because the mind cannot take these steps too rapidly. One has to build up the capacity to use many forms of reasoning. You do not sit down and read Nāgārjuna cover to cover; if you did, you would feel literally nauseated, become mentally sick, and lose all sense of practicality. It must be remembered that practicality is the most important thing, and indeed there is a practical reason for Nāgārjuna's setting forth so many reasonings on emptiness: providing more avenues for approaching emptiness in order to broaden the mind and thus bring about the destruction of the obstructions to omniscience and thereby attain buddhahood for the sake of all sentient beings.

When the great masters of Tibet talk about how to realize emptiness, they often speak of it from the viewpoint of merely one reasoning. In fact, they are using the Lesser Vehicle approach of limited reasoning, but this does not mean they are of the Lesser Vehicle. By being well accustomed to one form, you can build up the mental force to use many forms of analysis. To enhance this, you can picture your guru in front of you and make a prayer petition, "May I in the future have the ability to analyze in many different ways." Then imagine that you receive from her sustaining rays of colored ambrosia—white, red, green, blue, and yellow—that endow the continuum of your mind with this capacity. Get used to one type of analysis, and then go on to another, gradually expanding your capacity.

17. Thus, although there is no difference in the type of wisdom between the Lesser and Great Vehicles, there is a difference in the mode of cultivation and the eventual effect.

The wisdom consciousness of a Great Vehicle practitioner is capable of eradicating the obstructions to omniscience, whereas that of a Lesser Vehicle practitioner is not. This comes not only by way of the difference in method—motivation and its accompanying deeds—but also by way of the difference in the mode of cultivating wisdom, using limitless analyses or mainly one.

Frequently, it is said that one should not teach emptiness because people so easily misunderstand it. There is a great danger either of rejecting it out of a sense that phenomena inherently exist or of falling into nihilism by mistakenly thinking that emptiness means that phenomena do not exist at all. Only people who have predispositions from the past favorable for realizing emptiness or people who accept the assertion that dependent-arisings and emptiness are compatible.are suitable vessels of the teaching.

You may very well catch yourself thinking, "Then, nothing exists" or "There is only emptiness" and have to correct your understanding. Unsuitable people, however, would go much further, insisting that Dzong-ka-ba taught that dependent-arising is nothing and refusing to hear any more on the subject. They would not even allow someone to bring out a book by Dzong-ka-ba and read relevant passages. Their minds are closed. To such people emptiness should not be taught.

It is not the engaging in limitless reasonings that lengthens the bodhisattva path, for although it would take time to develop the capacity to use all the reasonings in Nāgārjuna's twenty-seven chapters, it would by no means take countless great eons. Their path is longer than that of Lesser Vehicle practitioners because in accumulating the merit that will empower their wisdom consciousness—practicing, for instance, never to refuse to bestow a gift out of miserliness or never to refuse to give teaching out of laziness—they are bringing about a far more thorough reformation of the basic mental attitude by transforming it into one of altruism than do Lesser Vehicle practitioners. They make an effort to help each and every person, learning how to discriminate between their qualities and faults, but never valuing them more or less on that basis.

If, while looking outside, we suddenly saw billows of smoke pouring from underneath the window, we would know incontrovertibly that there was a fire there. Despite not seeing the fire directly, we would have no doubt that it was there. This correct conviction would be founded on our thorough familiarity with the fact that the presence of smoke always indicates the presence of fire. It only takes an instant to perceive the smoke and conclude there is a fire; we are not left mulling over a series of reasons: "Wherever there is smoke there is fire, and over here we have smoke, so there must be a fire." Our inference that fire is nearby carries as much force as directly perceiving the flames.

The mind that realizes the presence of fire due to perceiving smoke is an inferential consciousness. It is conceptual but does not involve a lot of thought. It is explicit knowledge. It is similarly possible to have an inferential realization of emptiness that is an extremely powerful insight. The Dalai Lama has said that even the conceptual understanding of emptiness that *precedes* inference is like being struck by lightning. Such praise of conceptuality is revealing. We tend to believe that, although thought may be useful in making a food budget or buying proper books, it is of no help at all in determining and actually realizing the nature of reality.

Words cannot describe anything—much less reality—exactly as it is experienced. This is a well-known fact emphasized by both the upper and lower tenet systems. Nevertheless, in the Middle Way School, verbal reasoning is an important part of the path, because through it one can come to vivid decisions about emptiness just as one can unhesitatingly determine the presence of fire through seeing smoke. The point, then, is to use thought to determine confidently that things do not exist the way they appear. In this way, one can gain understanding of the absence of such inherently existent objects, of the voidness of such a status of existence. It is not that the things we see do not exist at all but rather that they do not exist as we perceive them. Getting used to this brings you, in time, to a non-conceptual understanding of emptiness.

Conceptual realization of emptiness is incontrovertible, and the object being realized is just emptiness. You can begin by observing that, for example, a table is a dependent-arising that arises, that is to say, is established, in dependence on its parts. Whatever arises in dependence on its parts does not exist inherently; it does not exist concretely as we perceive it to. It takes a long time to understand this. You must take care to recognize that we do, in fact, perceive things to have a concrete, inherent mode of existence, for then you can appreciate the relevance of the thought of dependent-arising with respect to specific objects. For example, a table arises in dependence on its parts—legs, top, nails, and so forth—and there is no whole table that exists separately from these parts. Since the table is a dependent-arising and since all dependent-arisings lack inherent existence, the table does not inherently exist.

When you perceive this thoroughly, you see the emptiness of inherent existence; this is an experience in which something very specific is understood. You are no longer mulling things over; you are just understanding emptiness. Your consciousness ascertains the absence of the inherent existence of the table. Only a vacuity appears. You are no longer observing the basis of the designation "table"; the brown color, square shape, and so forth no longer even appear. If I had a dog and decided to look for it, it would not take me too long to decide that it was not in this room. I would have a definite understanding of its absence. In a similar way, when realizing the emptiness of the inherent existence of a table, only that vacuity that is the negative of inherent existence appears. You began with a definite sense of a concrete table and then analyze to see if it is actually there or not. Finding the non-findability of such a concrete table, or realizing the emptiness of such a table, is the fruit of your analysis.

We have at present a strong sense of a concrete table despite the fact that there is no such thing. Its appearance is a total deception. After searching for it and not finding it, we pay attention only to the absence of this solid thing we were looking for. At that time, we are not, with part of our mind, noting some type of conventionally existent table that is not negated. The fact that only the table's *emptiness* of inherent existence appears is a measure of how strong that conceptual realization is. What makes it conceptual and not direct is the fact that an *image* of emptiness is appearing. Cognition of an object through the medium of an image is considered to be conceptual although we would probably think of it as direct cognition. We would probably describe an inferential realization of emptiness as an intuition because the feeling content is so strong. Or, we might consider it an intellectual intuition because, being based on valid reasons, it is incontrovertible, whereas ordinary intuition is not.

Many people who analyze in this way reach a point in their meditation where everything clears out and they therefore conclude that nothing exists. This is wrong. Correctly done, this analysis leads to a *specific* vacuity, not a blanket nothingness. It is specific both in terms of what appears and what is ascertained. If you began by investigating the inherent existence of a certain table, you would understand the lack of *inherent* existence—not of *any* mode of existence—of that table. The lack of inherent existence is thus not nothingness, even if, at that time, the object whose emptiness is being perceived is no longer appearing.

Having understood a specific instance of the absence of inherent existence, you can then apply it to all other phenomena. Finally, when just the vacuity that is a negative of inherent existence appears, and your mind becomes fused with it such that even the subtlest trace of a sense of subject and object vanishes, you have a direct realization of emptiness. Because this high state is non-conceptual, many people feel that right now we should put aside thought and conception altogether. They are quite mistaken; they have not understood the breadth and possibilities of conceptual thinking and are simply exasperated with the fruitlessness of the mulling over of ideas that they equate with conceptuality. True enough, thought has to be controlled and directed until it is brought to the point of this special type of conceptual realization—which, it is worth repeating, is only conceptual in the sense that you are realizing emptiness through the medium of an image and not nakedly. Getting used to this realization within the context of a stable and alert consciousness causes the conceptual realization itself to turn into direct realization. The sense of subject (the wisdom consciousness) and object (emptiness) gradually diminishes, and the mind and emptiness become like fresh water poured into fresh water. Therefore, those who say that conceptual thought must be abandoned now are turning their backs on the means of actually getting beyond conceptuality. The way to overcome erroneous conceptual thought is to use correct conceptual thought, for the latter burns up the former and in the process consumes itself. The *Kāshyapa Chapter (’od srungs kyi le’u, kāśyapaparivarta)* says:[37]

> Kāshyapa, it is thus: For example, fire arises when the wind rubs two branches together. Once the fire has arisen, the two branches are burned. Just so Kāshyapa, if you have the correct analytical intellect, a Superior's faculty of wisdom is generated. Through its generation, the correct analytical intellect is consumed.

Eventually, you are left just with direct realization of the truth.[38] Conceptuality must be kept in its place—one would not prefer it to direct realization—but it is an essential part of the path.

Dzong-ka-ba emphasizes that not appreciating the value of conceptuality is a chief cause of undermining the spiritual path. Nevertheless, he says that a conceptual understanding of emptiness is not able to overcome any obstructions. It must be conjoined with a mind of great concentration called calm abiding and then enhanced by alternating stabilizing and analytical meditation. Even then, this combination is not sufficient to overcome obstructions; realization conjoined with this power of concentration must be brought to the point of *direct* realization of emptiness that marks the beginning of the path of seeing.

The *innate* conception of inherent existence as well as the *innate* desire, hatred, and so forth that arise because of it are not based on anything that you have learned or concluded through reasoning. Even small children have an innate sense of an inherently existent "I." They might begin to wonder whether that "I" exists in this or that part of his body, whether it extends throughout it or is perhaps no larger than the smallest thing they can imagine. Once they have reached this point in reflection, they would have made up an artificial system, based on innate misconception but developed by analysis. Even animals are born with a mistaken sense of an inherently existent "I," and their activities of searching for food, fighting, and so on are mixed with this error, as are our own.

Those who advocate casting aside thought do so on the presupposition that our minds are basically good—that if it were not for the interference of thought, we could experience things directly, just as they are. This type of Buddhism does not agree, for the obstructions to omniscience as described in the Consequence School are the false *appearance* of phenomena to the sense and mental consciousnesses. Thus, even the non-conceptual senses are polluted, not by present thought but by predispositions established by actions in the past. Thus, even in terms of direct perception, we do not have so much as a single moment of correct perception of the nature of phenomena.

A conceptual realization of emptiness is incontrovertible. When it is conjoined with the altruistic aspiration to enlightenment, you achieve the middling level of a bodhisattva's path of accumulation. When this realization of emptiness is conjoined with the force of calm abiding, and then analytical and stabilizing meditation are alternated until analysis itself induces greater stability and meditative stability induces a greater capacity for analysis, the path of preparation is attained. This harmonious union of mutually supportive stabilizing and analytical meditation on emptiness is known as special insight.

Throughout the path of preparation, emptiness is realized through the medium of an image, but on the path of seeing it is realized directly for the first time, whereupon the intellectually acquired, or artificial, obstructions to liberation are overcome. These consist of misconceptions that have been acquired through training—school, church, reading, and so forth—that have affirmed or increased your sense of inherent existence. Although such errors are learned, we grow so accustomed to them that it is as if they were spontaneous. All afflictive emotions built on such artificial affirmation are immediately destroyed upon reaching the path of seeing. They will never return, either in this lifetime or a future one. The generation of the consciousness that is their actual antidote marks the beginning of the path of seeing and, simultaneously, the beginning of the first bodhisattva ground.

However, the innate afflictive emotions, which you have had since beginningless time, are not yet destroyed; they are merely dormant during the meditative equipoise that directly realizes emptiness. If you drop a very dirty garment into soapy water, the grossest dirt comes out right away. Similarly, the coarsest afflictive emotions—artificial ones—are overcome first. Then, through entering into direct realization over and over again, the mind is empowered to overcome the innate afflictive emotions. When your mind becomes able to eliminate the grossest of the gross *innate* afflictive emotions, you have attained the path of meditation. All levels of the innate afflictive emotions are gradually overcome by the beginning of the eighth bodhisattva ground. After this, you begin to vanquish the obstructions to omniscience.

Even before conceptuality has time to operate, as in the very first moment of an eye consciousness perceiving a wall, error is present. Nevertheless, it is worthwhile to become familiar with the sense of concretely appearing objects that occurs even at the sensory level, for then you are in a position to identify the "self"—inherent existence—that is negated in the view of selflessness. It is startling to comprehend that the very appearance of phenomena to direct perception is mistaken. This mistake is due to a fault in the perceiving consciousness, not in the object perceived. Still, it is not a defect arising from the *present* conceptual process. We can, therefore, conclude without any hesitation that the systemization of the Middle Way School in Tibet by Dzong-ka-ba and so forth is not merely a call to tune into direct perception by destroying conceptuality.

Some writers claim that the Middle Way School is primarily concerned with refuting other systems of thought. This is not the case.

The Middle Way School does give a fair amount of attention to pointing out errors in other Buddhist and non-Buddhist tenet systems, but the reason for doing so is that these systems reinforce the various mistakes that exist in our own minds, founded on the mistaken conception of inherent existence. Dzong-ka-ba says that the refutation of mistaken systems of thought is a branch of the refutation of the innate conception of inherent existence.

Most meditation systems in the world are basically methods of increasing mental stability. The Middle Way School does teach the necessity of calming the mind before engaging in analytical meditation; it involves as much meditative stabilization as any other religious system, but it teaches that reality will not be realized through such methods alone. Many unusual appearances may occur; one may get a sense that the mind is piercing through objects. This is insight of a sort but not the means of getting out of cyclic existence. For that, it is necessary to cultivate special insight into emptiness. After you have stilled your mind sufficiently to crystallize a sense of how things are appearing, you investigate whether that appearance is deceptive or not. Unless the mind is somewhat still, it is impossible to identify how things appear. For a night watchman to do his job properly, he must keep his eyes open; similarly, in order for analysis to hit the appearances that are its mark, the meditator must perceive them clearly.

Interpreters of the Middle Way School who hold that liberation is simply a matter of gaining awareness of non-conceptual sense perception and non-conceptual mental perception maintain that the essential insight of Nāgārjuna's teaching is that words are inadequate. They say that only an undue reliance on words, which are not able to express experience, gets us into trouble. Such a view is an undervaluation of the Middle Way School, for the inability of words fully to express their objects is detailed in the Sūtra School system. A word such as "table" cannot cause an actual table with all its particular characteristics to appear to your mind. So too the word "emptiness" will not cause you to realize reality. The Middle Way School agrees with the Sūtra School on this, but Nāgārjuna's insight goes deeper. The target that his reasoning sets out to destroy is our unembellished sense of tables as concrete and findable. The sense of such inherent existence is with us all the time and is so much a part of our experience that it is necessary to still the mind even to identify its appearance.

Once the target—the sense of inherent existence—has been set up, the second step is to consider the relationship between the table and its parts. If the table is as concrete an entity as it seems to be, there is a finite number of relationships that can obtain between them. For example, you can conclude either that the table and its parts are the same or they are different. Nāgārjuna himself *limited* the number of possibilities that one need consider and did not merely argue against positions that other systems held at the time. If he had, he could not have concluded definitely that all phenomena lack inherent existence but would still be waiting to see if someone else might come up with another possibility that he would then try to refute. Rather, Nāgārjuna sets up all the possibilities and refutes them one by one. According to Ďzong-ka-ba, Nāgārjuna does not claim that we innately conceive any of these positions to be true but that one of them *would have to be* the case if things existed the way they appear. It is implicit that the mind is sufficiently powerful to come to a conclusion, namely, to limit the number of positions to be refuted and comprehend that if none of these is suitable, the appearance of inherent existence must be false.

We face many similar situations in daily life. Take, for example, a criminal investigation in which a great deal of evidence begins to accumulate against a politician accused of embezzling funds. Despite the mounting evidence against him, when the accused appears on television and says, "I am innocent," he may be very convincing. In order not to be taken in by his pleasing appearance and sincere manner it is necessary to rely on reasoned analysis. A person who is not an embezzler does not receive money in illegal ways. Knowing this, one could analyze his funding and decide whether or not his claim could bear analysis. Once you decide on the criteria for being a criminal, anyone who does not measure up must be considered a criminal, no matter how honest he or she appears.

If raw sensation were correct and only conceptuality and analysis were sources of error, animals would not be caught in cyclic existence.

Nāgārjuna's analysis is not meant to mirror an innate analytical decision, for no one spontaneously takes the position that a table is either the same as or different from its parts. Nevertheless, if a table exists as it so concretely appears, there are only a certain number of possibilities that can ensue, and in refuting these Nāgārjuna shows that basic appearance is mistaken. It is quite backward to conclude that only words mislead, for on such a basis it would be difficult to posit any spiritual path.

Important as stabilization and analysis are in understanding reality, other practices are also a significant part of the path. One's attitude toward one's spiritual guide can aid progress. By offering everything you find desirable to your teacher, it is possible to relieve yourself of much distraction due to attachment. Once you have offered everything you might crave, you can offer the entire universe until the mind is emptied of all objects of desire, and you are left with a sense of infinite space. In this way you achieve a greater freedom of mind. For example, if you are someone who constantly hungers for chocolate cake, you can mentally offer hundreds of thousands of chocolate cakes to your teacher until it happens that as soon as one appears to your mind it is simply absorbed into her or him. You are free of it. You are closer to raw direct perception, for involvement with this type of desire *further* concretizes false appearance. One reason writers on Buddhism despise thought is because they notice that the mind becomes uncontrolled when thought takes over. We lose a sense of the stuff of things and become more distanced from the false appearance by adding thought in the form of desire, nervousness, anxiety, and so forth. Yet, thought is not useless; it must be controlled to serve its purpose, and techniques for using it correctly are an essential part of Buddhist practice.

Both Hinduism and Buddhism have practices that culminate in an expansive non-dualistic cognition. Hindus who search for Brahman identify everything that appears to their mind as *not* Brahman: The mind is not Brahman; the eyes, ears, nose are not; the trees are not; and so forth. Eventually you become accustomed to this cancellation of appearances to the point where things no longer appear. What remains at that time is Brahman; it is identified as your true self.

Thereby, in Vedānta you come to cancel the notion that Brahman is far away and that the *jīva*—the personality you normally identify with—is afflicted or limited in any manner. The true nature of the self is understood to be the pure, unchanging Brahman, the inner essence of your being. You have a non-dualistic cognition of Brahman as fused with the self and as the nature of everything in the universe. Nothing but Brahman appears to the mind.

In Buddhism, you begin by researching the nature of phenomena, patiently searching for the concretely existing table or, more likely, your body, or mind, or the "I" that you identified as the target to be investigated. Eventually, a vacuity of such a table appears, and even during such conceptual realization of emptiness, you do not ascertain a sense of yourself as the cognizing subject. Then, when emptiness is directly cognized, there is no sense of subject-object differentiation whatsoever. Nothing appears except the emptiness that is a vacuity of inherent existence.

It would be a great mistake and an impediment to their own progress for Buddhists to badmouth the vastness and immediacy of the Vedāntin realization, for the insight Buddhists seek is also vast and immediate. Yet important differences do exist. To realize Brahman, you put aside appearances as if turning the head away from them. The Buddhist practitioner in a sense does the opposite; she zeros in on phenomena to investigate them more closely and eventually perceives a reality, or emptiness, that is the same entity as the phenomenon it qualifies. Emptiness is seen as the very stuff of appearance and a necessary condition for it. This is different from Vedānta, where you realize a great entity that cancels out the reality of smaller entities. Yet there is a similarity in tone. For example, in Buddhist tantra, after you have searched to find the person and realized its emptiness, you cause the very mind that is fused with that emptiness to appear as a deity.

One of the great problems in researching emptiness is the tendency of the mind to scatter when it engages in conceptual thought. People then conclude that conceptual thought is the enemy to be overcome, but this is not so. The point is to make conceptuality and stabilization work together.

14. THE TWO GREAT VEHICLES

Everything that characterizes the Great Vehicle in general applies equally to both its vehicles—Perfection and Mantra. These two can then be contrasted within the context of their similarities. As before, they must be distinguished in the sense of being vehicles *to* which or *by* which one progresses or both.

Because the goal of both the Perfection (or Sūtra) and Mantra (or Tantra) Great Vehicles is the same—buddhahood—they do not differ as vehicles in terms of that to which one progresses, as do the Lesser and Great Vehicles. The same type of buddhahood is described by both. More specifically, as Jam-ȳang-shay-b̄a[39] points out, some Great Vehicle sūtras state that a buddha's body is solid, without openings, and that a buddha does not breathe. Similarly, in highest yoga tantra, buddhahood is described as a state in which all coarse levels of wind *(rlung, prāṇa),* or breath, have ceased, the very subtle mind of clear light has become manifest, and the wind that serves as its mount is used as the substance of pure body in a state of continual and simultaneous meditative equipoise and appearance. Furthermore, sūtra describes buddhahood as a condition of having overcome the obstructions to liberation and omniscience. One is omniscient and able to realize the two truths simultaneously and directly; one has overcome all faults and perfected all good qualities. How could the buddhahood of tantra be a state beyond this? It is not.

One complication is the assertion that although buddhahood can be attained through the practice of the Perfection Vehicle, it is not possible to attain it through the Perfection Vehicle *alone.* It is said that through sūtra one can approach the end of the tenth bodhisattva ground but cannot complete it. One must utilize highest yoga tantra to attain buddhahood. The first of the ten bodhisattva grounds begins at the path of seeing. The second through the tenth comprise the path of meditation, and the eleventh ground, which is simultaneous with the path of no more learning, is buddhahood, the ground of complete light. By engaging in the practices of the Perfection Vehicle alone you can approach buddhahood but cannot achieve it. So, some have felt that, because through the Perfection Vehicle alone one cannot achieve buddhahood, the fruit it describes differs from that of tantra. Nevertheless, the two vehicles do *describe* the same type of buddhahood, and for this reason there is no difference between the two in terms of the vehicle as that to which one progresses.

The Perfection and Mantra Vehicles differ because of the *means* used to attain that fruit. In turn, the means or practices for achieving buddhahood are all included in method and wisdom; thus the differences in the two vehicles must lie in one or both of these.

In general, the two Great Vehicles do not differ in wisdom for the same reasons that the Lesser and Great Vehicles do not. For there is no mode of subsistence[40] of phenomena more subtle than the emptiness taught by Nāgārjuna. There is, however, a more subtle consciousness realizing it than that taught in the Perfection Vehicle; furthermore, this type of consciousness is not common to all four tantras but unique to highest yoga tantra.

Due to the difference in the viewing consciousness and due to the fact that this consciousness is fused with the emptiness it realizes, the Ñying-ma-ɓa order says that there is a difference in view between the two higher vehicles. The Ge-luk-ɓa order, referring only to the "objective" clear light—that is to say, the emptiness that is the object being realized—says that the two vehicles do not differ in terms of wisdom.

There actually seems to be no contradiction between the orders on this point, for the Ge-luk-ɓas also set forth the subtle consciousnesses of highest yoga tantra but, unlike the Ñying-ma-ɓas, do not hold that a difference in consciousness constitutes a difference in view. Since emptiness and the consciousness realizing it are utterly fused, the

Ñying-ma-ḃas have good reason for considering the achievement of a much subtler consciousness—the combination of viewing consciousness (or subjective view) and object viewed (or objective view)—a difference in view. In Dzong-ka-ḃa's presentation, since the two higher vehicles do not differ in terms of wisdom with respect to the emptiness that is realized by a wisdom consciousness, the two vehicles must be distinguished only by way of a difference in method.

The Mantra Vehicle itself contains many methods, as does the Perfection Vehicle. The method that constitutes the distinction between these two Vehicles, however, cannot be merely the various techniques used by fast and slow bodhisattvas, for example, since even within the Perfection Vehicle there are such differences. Nor can this difference have to do with the altruistic aspiration to enlightenment, for this is the fundamental Great Vehicle practice that is common to both the Perfection and Mantra Vehicles. The bodhisattva deeds—the six perfections—which have altruistic aspiration as their basis, are also common to both.

A buddha has two bodies, a truth body and a form body. The omniscient consciousness and its emptiness comprise the truth body, and a buddha's various types of appearances—pure, impure, obstructive, and non-obstructive—comprise the form body. The main means for bringing about the truth body is the collection of wisdom and that for bringing about the form body is the collection of merit. Although the truth body is the chief imprint of wisdom and the form body is the chief imprint of method, there cannot be one without the other. They are attained simultaneously, and both collections are required to attain buddhahood.

Of the two buddha bodies, bodhisattvas are mainly intent upon achieving the form body. Through it they will be able to complete the primary purpose of helping sentient beings since the form body can appear to other beings, teach what is to be adopted in practice, and so forth in myriad ways appropriate to those trainees. Mantra contains a significantly different additional technique—deity yoga—for achieving the form body. It is this practice that distinguishes the Mantra Vehicle from the Perfection Vehicle. Deity yoga is the special method practiced in addition to the altruistic aspiration to enlightenment and the bodhisattva deeds induced by it.

It is important to recognize clearly that the special features of tantra are *in addition* to the bodhisattva ideals; thus, any discussion of using sexual desire and so forth in tantra is neither contrary to nor a substitute for the wish to achieve others' happiness, even if the terms "compassion" and "mind of enlightenment" are *sometimes* used to refer to bliss and essential bodily fluids. Rather, it is a means of allowing certain highly qualified people to achieve altruistic buddhahood more quickly than would otherwise be possible, by utilizing the subtler, blissful consciousnesses associated with sexual union and so forth to realize emptiness. The Mantra Vehicle is faster for one who is a suitable practitioner of it than the Perfection Vehicle would be for the same person, but it is not faster for everyone. If a person unsuited to tantra attempts to practice it, his or her path to buddhahood could be lengthened greatly.

Deity yoga is a special means for generating a union of calm abiding and special insight. It enables completion of the paths of accumulation and preparation in a single lifetime rather than the period of countless great eons that Sūtra Great Vehicle techniques require. This is how the Dalai Lama describes the speed of the tantric method.[41]

As Dzong-ka-ba says, the attainment of buddhahood in one short lifetime of the degenerate era—about fifty to one hundred years—is not a feature of tantra in general because such is possible only through practice of highest yoga tantra. It may, through the lower tantras, be possible to achieve buddhahood in one lifetime because certain yogis can extend their lives over many eons. Thus, they can practice highest yoga tantra and achieve buddhahood within that long life, but such cannot be called a short lifetime of the degenerate era. Lower tantras sometimes claim that they are final and that buddhahood can be achieved through them alone, but this is to be interpreted as an exaggerated expression of such tantras' greatness.[42]

Certain Nying-ma-ba texts state the possibility of achieving buddhahood through the three lower tantras within one lifetime; nevertheless, the Nying-ma-bas do not actually practice these except as preliminaries to their techniques of highest yoga tantra. They are not dismayed by the contradictions involved in saying that buddha-hood is possible through the lower tantras. Because such is said in the texts, they maintain it as true, but in terms of actual practice it is disregarded.

In a sense, Ñying-ma-ɓa explanations are not as smoothly interwoven as those of Dzong-ka-ɓa who, it can be said, orders the stages of the Ge-luk-ɓa path in terms of that path's entire spectrum. The explanations of the lower stages flow concordantly into those of the latter. In the Ñying-ma-ɓa path structure, new views are taught as your capacity increases. Their system teaches nine vehicles, or path-systems, which are unified in the sense that all could be generated gradually within the mental continuum of a single person. However, they are not unified in the sense that the lower are explained in such a way that they do not contradict the final teaching. The Ge-luk-ɓa presentation, however, is of *concordant* gradations. For this reason, the general presentation of the Ge-luk-ɓa path by Dzong-ka-ɓa is more esoteric than the general Ñying-ma-ɓa presentation because Dzong-ka-ɓa takes account of the highest view from the very beginning.

To exaggerate this distinction a bit, in Ñying-ma it is as if the individual levels contradict each other as you advance, whereas in Ge-luk there is a harmony from beginning to end—the end affecting how the beginning is presented. In Ñying-ma when the final, valid vehicle is presented, one has the sense that buddhas are reaching down and pulling you up to their level by describing what their own state is like, whereas in Ge-luk, through a harmonious presentation of the whole path, the *gradations* of practice and experience take on more significance. There are advantages to both presentations.

The main practitioners of the four tantras are distinguished by their ability to use the bliss that arises from different types of desire in the path. Looking or gazing (action tantra), laughing or smiling (performance tantra), embracing or holding hands or touching other parts of the body such as the breasts (yoga tantra), and union of the sexual organs (highest yoga tantra) are the four increasingly powerful (and increasingly challenging) activities within which one trains. For example, someone meditating on impermanence tries to maintain her understanding of it during various daily activities. You try to maintain it in an exceedingly pleasant place, in a place that is frightening, and, finally, you might try to keep it in mind while holding hands with a girlfriend or boyfriend. The point would be to maintain the continuum of understanding impermanence within the context of the happiness that arises through contact with pleasurable circumstances. This would become more and more difficult as the pleasure increased.

It is said that there are beings in other realms who find complete satisfaction when males and females merely look at each other, or smile at each other, or merely embrace. In our own realm these three plus sexual union are necessary for full satisfaction. The four tantras can be divided on the basis of their main trainees' capacities in bringing such desirous activities to the path. The main trainees of action tantra are those able to use the bliss arising from the desire associated with looking at each other. This does not mean that *all* trainees of action tantra are able to do so, but the practitioners for whom action tantra was mainly and specifically taught are described this way. Such people can use this blissful consciousness to realize emptiness, thereby eventually overcoming all desire including that associated with holding hands; they are not reinforcing it. Just as, according to a Buddhist example, bugs that are generated from moist wood consume that wood, so, the bliss arising from desire is itself part of the process of overcoming desire when it is used to realize emptiness. As the Dalai Lama says, if you do not have the capacity for this, leave it alone.[43] In other words, do not claim that, when you hold hands and so forth, it is part of the path. Many people have not understood this important point.

Tantric techniques for enhancing method and wisdom can, for unscrupulous people, open the door to many activities that should not be done. Promiscuity is not tantra although some people might try to justify their pleasure-seeking by saying that it is—"Come to my place, and we'll practice tantra."

Tantric practice is also not a case of overcoming excessive interest in nonvirtue by engaging in it for a while. This may be a side advantage inasmuch as it is sometimes helpful to do something you always wanted to do—as long as it harms no one—and thereby free your mind of it. If someone is attached to sleep, let him sleep for a week until he is fed up with it. Normally, however, the satisfaction of a desire quells it only for a short time; soon you are off for another pizza or chocolate cake. In tantra, desire is used to overcome desire in the sense that the desire involved in looking, laughing, holding hands or embracing, and the union of male and female organs is used to generate a *strong, blissfully withdrawn* consciousness that then realizes the emptiness of inherent existence, which, when thoroughly understood, makes desire impossible.

In brief, some have said that the tantric practitioner engages in activities of desire in order to become tired of them. However, merely engaging in an activity to the point of revulsion does not generate a blissful consciousness that can be used—because of its power—in the path.

Clarifying this distinction makes it possible to recognize how difficult tantric practice is and how important it is to realize your present level of capacity. By hearing about these higher reaches of the path you can understand the significance of the lower stages as necessary precursors to them. For example, hearing that tantra involves desirous activities done within an understanding of emptiness lets you know that it is necessary to understand emptiness. How can we do that? Meditation on impermanence is conducive to the realization of emptiness. Thus, by understanding that desire eventually is used in the path for realizing emptiness with a special consciousness, a beginner can realize the necessity and importance of meditation on impermanence. Letting the most esoteric teachings filter down through the beginning stages of the path in this way enables the practitioner to appreciate the early practices; you can understand that they are *integral* parts of the later practices. It is then easy to be willing to take the time and effort to achieve the beginning stages of the path. Otherwise, our pride is such that we become impatient, wanting to get to the higher practices. Those who know that the preceding practices are not external to tantra but integral parts of it know that, in a sense, they are practicing tantra simply by making an endeavor at what is suitable for them at present. This is how to build up the causes for practicing tantra; one finds the inspiration to do so partly through knowing what the special features of tantra are.

> *18. The two Great Vehicles, the Perfection Vehicle and the Mantra Vehicle, have the same fruit and the same wisdom; therefore, the difference lies in method, which is tantra's special feature of deity yoga.*

The names of the two vehicles might lead you to think that in mantra the perfections are discarded. This is not so; rather, the Mantra Vehicle is distinguished by adding something further to them.

> *19. A practitioner of tantra must have particularly intense compassion, being in great haste to become a buddha in order to help others.*

One does not enter tantra out of an unwillingness to spend three periods of countless great eons on the path. Practitioners of tantra would be ready to spend this amount of time but, because of their wish to help others as quickly as possible, seek a shorter path. Tantra is not, as some think, a less taxing technique given to inferior practitioners who cannot bear the rigors of the Perfection Vehicle. As practiced nowadays, it is not necessary actually to be a bodhisattva—to have fully generated an altruistic intention to become enlightened—to receive tantric initiation, but the recipient must be someone for whom helping others is very important and who is making an effort to become a bodhisattva.

> *20. Method in the Perfection and Mantra Vehicles is the same with respect to the basis of practice, which is the altruistic intention to become enlightened, and the deeds of practice, which are the perfections of giving, ethics, and patience. Therefore, the Mantra Vehicle does not discard or transcend the conventional mind of enlightenment (the aspiration to achieve enlightenment for the sake of all beings and the bodhisattva deeds) or the ultimate mind of enlightenment (direct realization of emptiness by a bodhisattva). However, mantra has the additional feature of deity yoga.*

The time of fully generating a conventional mind of enlightenment—the altruistic intention to become enlightened—is simultaneous with the beginning of the path of accumulation. A learner's ultimate mind of enlightenment is a bodhisattva's path of seeing or path of meditation at the time when the wisdom consciousness directly realizes emptiness. Such a mind of enlightenment is called ultimate because its object is the ultimate, emptiness. The ultimate mind of enlightenment does not cancel out the conventional one: A buddha has both. A buddha's wish that others attain highest enlightenment—buddhahood—is a conventional mind of enlightenment; it deals with conventional phenomena, namely, people.

21. *The difference in speed between the two Great Vehicles is due to a faster accumulation of merit in the Mantra Vehicle (if one is capable of practicing it), resulting from the cultivation of deity yoga. This involves meditation cultivating a similitude of a buddha's residence, form body, resources, and activities.*

A buddha's bodies can be enumerated as two, three, four, or five, and these are all included in the two, truth and form bodies. In the Perfection Vehicle you cultivate a similitude of a buddha's truth body by entering meditative equipoise on emptiness. All appearances vanish, and the mind is fused with the emptiness of inherent existence. Perfection Vehicle meditators do not generate themselves in the body of a buddha or visualize themselves as residing in a buddha's mansion, but they do cultivate a state similar in aspect to the mind of a buddha (in terms of its realization of emptiness) in which the vacuity of inherent existence is all that appears, and the wisdom consciousness is fused with it. In mantra, this very consciousness itself is caused to appear in the form of a deity. This is deity yoga.

The wisdom consciousness, which is not form and not matter, appears as form. When it appears, the meditator is still meditating on emptiness; this is the union of method and wisdom in the Mantra Vehicle.

15. DEITY YOGA

Due to the practice of deity yoga, the union of method and wisdom achieved in mantra is different from that of sūtra. The compassionate appearance of the wisdom consciousness itself in the form of a buddha performing altruistic deeds is method—wisdom and method being thereby contained within one consciousness. Since an actual buddha has both a form body and a truth body, the supreme means of achieving buddhahood is to engage in practice that is similar in aspect to these right now. The practice is difficult because it is necessary first to generate compassion, to have at least some understanding of emptiness, and then to cause that very consciousness that understands the absence of inherent existence to appear as a divine form within an understanding of emptiness.

In the Sūtra Great Vehicle, the six perfections are practiced in "limitless" ways over a "limitless" period of time, and there is no mention about generating (imagining) yourself as having the body of a buddha. You might practice calm abiding by stabilizing on a visualized buddha imagined in front of yourself, accustoming the mind to a buddha's appearance and mixing the mind with it, but you would not meditate on yourself as a buddha. Still, such visualization helps in developing the capacity for self-generation as a deity.

Because imagining yourself as a deity can be frightening as well as difficult, many paths for doing so are taught. Some people succeed at this practice only when it is accompanied by a great deal of ritual, rigorous cleanliness, and so forth. Others do not require these. In a similar way, for people unable to think about the subtlest emptiness, the Mind-Only system is taught; for those who can not benefit from this, the

Sūtra School and Great Exposition School systems are taught. People who cannot understand tenets of any type can benefit simply from keeping certain vows—even maintaining the refuge vow alone.

In the Perfection Vehicle, in order to unify method and wisdom you cultivate a buddha's truth body by realizing emptiness in such a way that the mind realizing emptiness is indistinguishable from emptiness. You then rise from this meditation in your ordinary body, and although the realization of emptiness itself is no longer there, the *force* of it remains such that you go about compassionate activities within its influence. The mind of compassion is conjoined with the force of the wisdom consciousness that realizes the absence of inherent existence. Similarly, you cultivate compassion in meditation such that a strong compassionate mind arises; then, when you enter meditation on emptiness, the *force* of that compassion—but not the mind of compassion itself—remains. In this sense, the wisdom that realizes emptiness is conjoined with, or affected by the force of, compassion.

In mantra, however, method and wisdom are actually and simultaneously present due to the compassionate appearance of the wisdom consciousness itself within ascertainment of the absence of inherent existence. Even now it is possible to experience what it is like for a consciousness to appear as a form. When you have succeeded in generating a certain degree of compassion upon going through the seven steps for generating the altruistic mind of enlightenment—recognition of all sentient beings as mothers, mindfulness of their kindness, developing a wish to repay their kindness, love, compassion, and the unusual altruistic attitude—observe the intense, compassionate mind itself and cause it to appear as a flat moon disc at your own heart. It is often said that the moon is a symbol of compassion, but here the moon is *composed* of compassion. This is not the same as visualizing something before you; the consciousness is being caused to appear as a certain object. Even if you cannot actually do this, it is said to be helpful to *imitate* it.

In the Perfection Vehicle, one does not achieve a union of method and wisdom in which compassion and wisdom are actually present in one consciousness. Nevertheless, if people like us were able to understand emptiness and, after rising from this meditation, proceeded to interact with people compassionately while the force of this realization remained, we would definitely feel that method and wisdom were both present in our continuums. It is no small thing for an activity to be conjoined with the force of an understanding of emptiness or the force of compassion. It is just that tantra has an even more profound type of unity wherein the realizational mind itself, out of compassion, appears as a deity. That very form is the aspect of compassionate method.

To know that deity yoga is the distinctive feature of tantra and to understand what it involves reinforces the structure of the entire path. It is clear that, for example, practicing calm abiding with a buddha's body as your object would be helpful because it accustoms you to the appearance of a buddha body. Knowing about deity yoga also shows the importance of carefully analyzing and studying emptiness. This in turn highlights the significance of identifying the phenomena of cyclic existence as having a nature of suffering and then realizing their impermanence. Compassion is also necessary for deity yoga, hence the necessity for cultivating altruism step by step, beginning with the equanimity toward neutral people, friends, and enemies that is the foundation on which the development of compassion must rest.

Often pride causes us to have interest only in the highest system; yet, if you really know what that system is and how the other practices lead directly to it, there is great satisfaction in cultivating the lower practices.

22. *Emptiness yoga is a general feature of Buddhist deity yoga, distinguishing it from non-Buddhist deity yoga.*

For example, Hindu religions have deity yoga but not emptiness yoga.

23. *In emptiness yoga one must confidently stabilize on the vacuity that is a negative of inherent existence found after searching for the concretely existent self that so palpably appears to us.*

Before practicing deity yoga, it is necessary to begin the process of understanding the emptiness of inherent existence. It is, first of all, necessary to clarify how an inherently or concretely existent "I" is conceived, to know its measure. Then you can determine that if such an "I" exists, it *must* be either inherently the same as or different from mind and body. This decision will later yield the confidence to stabilize on the vacuity that is the absence of such an "I," for once this is decided, the next step is to search for that concretely existent "I," and thorough investigation reveals that it cannot be found as either inherently the same as, or inherently different from, mind and body. At that point, a vacuity that is the absence of such an "I" appears.

Having perceived this vacuity, you stabilize on it. You do not just decide that nothing exists or that you cannot accurately discern the way things are. It is important to focus on the specific absence of a concretely existent self and let its significance seep deeply into the mind.

Moreover, the mind that realizes the emptiness of inherent existence is itself fused with that vacuity. Even for beginners, the sense of the mind as here and emptiness as somewhere over there starts to fade; the understanding of emptiness applies to the mind that searches for an inherently existent self as well as to that self. In direct realization of emptiness, subject and object are completely fused. The object of engagement is emptiness—not the "I" or mind or body—and the subject is the wisdom consciousness. Therefore, as a beginning practitioner, once you have some sense of unfindability, you might imitate the fusion of these two, for it would be a mistake to observe emptiness as something "over there," as if it had inherent existence.

Although the mind is fused with emptiness, you definitely retain an awareness of what is being realized. It is not observation free of content. It is not as if you have fallen into a dumb void or nothingness, or as if you had just been knocked out. This realization has a definite content despite the fact that it is a mode of cognition different from what we are accustomed to, for our perception is always dualistic. How do you come out of such a cognition if there is no dualistic mind to think, "Now I will finish realizing emptiness"? It is done by the power of your wish to reappear in order to help people.

Theravāda teaches that once buddhahood is achieved and the person subsequently dies, the person is no longer able to appear, but as far as the Great Vehicle is concerned, this is a mistake. Buddhas can and will return. This willingness and ability to reappear derive from the special Great Vehicle aspiration induced by love and compassion. Although Lesser Vehicle practitioners develop love and compassion for an immeasurable number of beings, beginning with understanding their own suffering and then extending this to friends, neutral people, and enemies, they do not have the bodhisattva's enthusiasm for investigating the lot of sentient beings. In fact, the Jay College of Śe-ra Monastic University in Tibet distinguishes the three types of love not by way of aspect—"How nice it would be if all sentient beings had happiness and its causes," "May all sentient beings have happiness and its causes," "I myself will join all sentient beings with happiness and its causes"—but from the viewpoint of the enthusiasm with which you engage in the object.[44]

The objects are all sentient beings, and bodhisattvas take great care to extend love and compassion to *all varieties* of beings. They extend it to beings in the north, south, east, and west, as well as the northeast, southeast, northwest, and southwest; then they consider beings in terms of, for example, Superiors and non-Superiors. In addition, bodhisattvas take the time to extend love and compassion to many, many individuals, to humans, to individual animals of every variety—friendly, neutral, and angry. Bodhisattvas also consider in detail the situations of gods, demigods, hungry ghosts, and hell beings. Such meditation requires great openness of mind and an enthusiasm for considering any sentient being's problems.

Jam-ȳang-shay-b̄a[45] says that, even though hearers and solitary realizers have *great* compassion in wishing that all beings be free from suffering, their compassion differs from that of bodhisattvas in many ways. It differs in vastness of object of observation because, even when taking cognizance of all sentient beings, hearers and solitary realizers do not go into the individual divisions of all beings but condense them. Thus their objects of observation are less vast. Also, since they wish only that all beings be free from suffering in general and do not take upon themselves the greater burden of protecting all beings from all faults (including the obstructions to omniscience), the subjective aspect of their compassionate consciousness is less. Also, since they do not meditate as repeatedly and with limitless analysis, their pangs of caring are less. For hearers and solitary realizers, the pangs of compassion are compared to the pain of fire touching the skin, whereas for bodhisattvas the comparison is to the pain of fire burning flesh. For these reasons, hearers' and solitary realizers' compassion is less than that of bodhisattvas in that they wish for reward for themselves, whereas bodhisattvas' compassion is for the sake of ripening, or developing, other beings. Also, the power of hearers' and solitary realizers' compassion is less than that of bodhisattvas such that they are discouraged about actions for helping others, whereas bodhisattvas are not. Hence, Jam-ȳang-shay-b̄a concludes that, even if hearers and solitary realizers have great compassion, it is a lesser form of it.

Perhaps it could be said that the difference between Lesser and Great Vehicle practitioners' cultivation of love and so forth is that the former practices with a sense of discouragement about cyclic existence to the extent that he or she is not enthusiastic in searching out more information on different types of sentient beings. The Great Vehicle practitioner, however, always relates to sentient beings from the viewpoint of great compassion, and thus involvement with them increases more and more.

It is important to recognize that just as an understanding of emptiness is compatible with appearance, so it is highly compatible with compassion. The selflessness of persons does not mean that there are no persons, or that there is no "I." It means that we misconceive the nature of that "I" in ourselves and others. There certainly are suffering people, and we must understand their conventional nature as well as their final mode of being. At the same time we should keep in mind that the impact of a realization of selflessness must be something like "I'm not at all what I thought I was" or "There isn't any 'I' at all!" Once we find out that the person does not inherently exist, that a person is like an illusion—appearing one way and existing another—it is possible to fall under the mistaken impression that we are refuting our very *existence*. At this point it is important to remember that people do exist, that they are valid and effective and suitable objects of compassion—that emptiness is compatible with dependent-arising.

If you love people and wish to help them and understand the compatibility of emptiness and appearance, why would you merely seek your own liberation from cyclic existence? In other words, why would anyone be a Lesser Vehicle practitioner? There are different personality types, and there are also unusual concentrations conjoined with special types of bliss by which one may become entranced, concentrations so deep and peaceful that one can remain in them for eons with no thought ever to rise from them.

However, from the Great Vehicle viewpoint it is indeed unthinkable not to help all these people with whom one has been so close in past lifetimes. They are like old friends fallen into a ravine and lying with their legs broken, and it would be terrible not to help them. This is quite different from the non-Great Vehicle perspective. There, the four immeasurables—love, compassion, joy, and equanimity—are cultivated to culminate not in compassion but in equanimity. One does develop strong good wishes for all living beings, but the resting point is an equanimity of non-involvement, without desire or hatred.

Nevertheless, the Theravāda tradition, for example, emphasizes that Buddha was active in teaching others after his own enlightenment. He did not simply practice the four immeasurables and then turn away from engagement with people. From the very beginning his motivation was to help. According to Theravāda, we cannot fully emulate Buddha; yet the foe destroyers, monks, and nuns of that tradition do emphasize teaching others. At the same time there remains in Theravāda a tension, verging on paradox, between the non-Great Vehicle presentation of persons as selfless and the ethic of benevolent involvement with them, because in Theravāda it looks as if selflessness is extended to mean that there are no people.

In the Ge-luk-ɓa interpretation of both the Lesser and Great Vehicle presentations of tenets, selflessness—that is, the lack of inherent existence—qualifies persons and all other phenomena, and thus persons and other phenomena must exist, even though the way that things appear to ordinary sight—as concretely or inherently existing— is not the way they actually exist. Also, emptinesses and objects are not different entities, and thus manifest appearance and activity are compatible with emptiness. Deity yoga is a technique that fosters an understanding of the mutuality of appearances—especially compassionate activity—and emptiness.

> 24. *Deity yoga involves causing the mind that realizes emptiness and is fused with that emptiness to appear itself as a deity, out of compassion, in order to help others.*

Although in the beginning stages one just imitates actual manifestation, there are people who can maintain deity yoga throughout the day. In all activities they are, to their own mental consciousness, appearing as a deity. The ability to carry pure appearance into all activities signifies stability in this practice. It is helpful to reflect that there are practitioners who have such ability; imagining this is one way to develop the capacity for doing so yourself.

> 25. *"Vajra" means an indivisible union of compassion and the wisdom that realizes emptiness.*

This is the general tantric meaning of "vajra." Thus, deity yoga itself—the appearance of a wisdom consciousness in the compassionate form of an enlightened being—is an instance of a vajra. In the practice of deity yoga, two things that might be considered separate—appearance and emptiness, or compassion and wisdom—are seen as one indivisible entity.

> 26. *The Perfection Vehicle does not have deity yoga even though it has meditation cultivating a similitude of the truth body, the spacelike meditative equipoise on emptiness.*
> 27. *All tantric practices are either deity yoga, emptiness yoga, or enhancers of these two.*
> 28. *The Perfection Vehicle alone is not sufficient for the attainment of buddhahood, nor are the three lower tantras alone. Highest yoga tantra is required for overcoming the extremely subtle obstructions to omniscience.*
> 29. *For tantra in general, the passage from the beginning of the path of accumulation to the path of seeing takes less time than the one period of countless great eons required in the Perfection Vehicle.*

Dzong-ka-b̄a does not explicitly make this distinction regarding the speed of tantra; this is the teaching of the present Dalai Lama.

> 30. *The attainment of buddhahood in one lifetime of this degenerate era is a distinctive feature of highest yoga tantra. Thus, the greater speed of Mantra over the Perfection Vehicle does not necessarily mean the attainment of buddhahood in one lifetime of this degenerate era.*

A lifetime of the degenerate era means a span of about a hundred years.

> 31. *Because the practices of the Perfection Vehicle are indispensable to and the very substance of the Mantra Vehicle, we should view even its ancillary practices, such as that of impermanence, which are conducive to realizing emptiness, as substantial contributors to the mantra path.*

The altruistic intention to become enlightened and so forth is not merely carried over *from* the Perfection Vehicle, they are *integral parts of* the Mantra Vehicle. Therefore, if you are practicing such altruism on the mantra path of accumulation, it is a mantra path.

Roughly speaking, it might be suitable to consider the mantra and perfection paths as large and small concentric circles, with the Perfection Vehicle contained within the Mantra Vehicle; everything the Perfection Vehicle has the Mantra Vehicle has. However, this diagram needs qualification since, for example, practicing the six perfections in limitless ways for a limitless period of time is distinctive to the Perfection Vehicle and is not part of the Mantra Vehicle.

These thirty-one points provide a significant grounding in the special features of tantra and its relation to the Great Vehicle and non-Great Vehicle systems. On the basis of this understanding you can read in more detail what Dzong-ka-b̄a or representatives of the other Tibetan orders—Ñying-ma, Ḡa-gyu, and S̄a-ḡya—have written about tantra and possess a sufficient background with which to absorb their meanings.

It has never been easy to gain access to the actual meaning of tantra; in that respect, what was true in ancient India and Tibet is perhaps even more the case today. After all, the tantras themselves sometimes seem to be anything but religious, with numerous passages that, on the surface at least, seem to be concerned with sexual esoterica. Also, some tantric texts give mantras and other techniques for overcoming enemies or for gaining objects of desire and so forth. Some people have, therefore, concluded that selfish pleasure and acquisition are the meaning and purpose of tantra. However, they have confused subsidiary practices—used with altruistic motivation to enhance the path—with the core of the path. The core is compassion and wisdom—a union of profound wisdom compassionately appearing in ideal form. The focus of this discussion and of the thirty-one essential points has been on the developed tantric tradition, the way it has been practiced for centuries in Tibet and the way it continues down to the present day in Tibetan communities.

GLOSSARY

(A Sanskrit entry marked with an asterisk is a reconstruction.)

English	Tibetan	Sanskrit
action	las	karma
action tantra	bya rgyud	kriyātantra
adventitious	glo bur ba	ākasmika
afflicted	nyon mongs can	kliṣṭa
afflicted self-cherishing	rang gces 'dzin nyon mongs can	
afflictive emotion	nyon mongs	kleśa
afflictive ignorance	nyon mongs can gyi ma rig pa	
afflictive obstruction	nyon sgrib	kleśāvaraṇa
aggregate	phung po	skandha
altruistic intention to become enlightened	byang chub kyi sems	bodhicitta
analysis	dpyod pa	vicāra
analytical meditation	dpyad sgom	
animal	dud 'gro	tiryañc
antidote	gnyen po	pratipakṣa
appearance	snang ba	pratibhāsa
appearance of inherent existence	rang bzhin gyis grub par snang ba	
appearance factor	snang cha	
Asaṅga	thogs med	asaṅga
ascertainment factor	nges cha	

aspect	rnam pa	ākāra
aspiration	'dun pa	chanda
aspirational mind of enlightenment	smon sems	
attachment	sred pa/chags pa	tṛṣṇa
Autonomy School	rang rgyud pa	svātantrika

basis of designation	gdags gzhi	
bliss	bde ba	sukha
bodhisattva	byang chub sems dpa'	bodhisattva
body	lus	kāya
body consciousness	lus kyi rnam shes	kāyavijñāna
buddha-lineage	sangs rgyas kyi rigs	buddhagotra

calm abiding	zhi gnas	śamatha
cause	rgyu	hetu
cessation	'gog pa	nirodha
clairvoyance	mngon shes	abhijña
clear light	'od gsal	prabhāsvara
coarse	rags pa	audārika
coarse selflessness of people	gang zag gi bdag med rags pa	
collection	tshogs	saṃbhāra
collection of merit	bsod nams kyi tshogs	puṇyasaṃbhāra
collection of wisdom	ye shes kyi tshogs	jñānasaṃbhāra
color	kha dog	varṇa
common being	so so skye bo	pṛthagjana
compassion	snying rje	karuṇā
complete enjoyment body	longs spyod rdzogs pa'i sku	saṃbhogakāya
concentration	bsam gtan	dhyāna
conception of inherent existence	rang bzhin gyis grub par 'dzin pa	*svabhāvasiddha-grāha
conceptuality	rnam rtog/rtog pa	vikalpa/kalpanā
concrete	ling nge ba	
conjoined	zin pa	

consciousness	shes pa/rnam shes	jñāna/vijñāna
Consequence School	thal 'gyur pa	prāsaṅgika
contaminated action	zag bcas kyi las	sāsravakarma
contaminated thing	zag bcas	sāsrava
contamination	zag pa	āsrava
continuum	rgyun/rgyud	saṃtāna
conventional mind of enlightenment	kun rdzob byang chub kyi sems	*saṃvṛtibodhicitta
conventional truth	kun rdzob bden pa	saṃvṛtisatya
conventionally existent	kun rdzob tu yod pa	saṃvṛtisat
cyclic existence	'khor ba	saṃsāra

---

defilement	sgrib pa	nivaraṇa
degenerate era	snyigs dus	
deity	lha	deva/devatā
deity yoga	lha'i rnal 'byor	*devayoga
demigod	lha ma yin	asura
dependent-arising	rten 'byung/rten 'brel/rten cing 'brel bar 'byung ba	pratītyasamutpāda
desire	'dod chags	rāga
desire realm	'dod khams	kāmadhātu
direct perception	mngon sum	pratyakṣa
direct realization	mngon sum du rtogs pa	pratyakṣa
doctrine	chos	dharma

---

ear consciousness	rna ba'i rnam shes	śrotravijñāna
effect	'bras bu	phala
effort	brtson 'grus	vīrya
emptiness	stong pa nyid	śūnyatā
enjoyment body	longs sku	saṃbhogakāya
enlightenment	byang chub	bodhi
entity	ngo bo	
equanimity	btang snyoms	upekṣā

established by way of its own character	rang gi mtshan nyid kyis grub pa	svalakṣaṇasiddha
established by way of its own entity	ngo bo nyid kyis grub pa	*svabhāvatāsiddha
ethics	tshul khrims	śīla
existent by way of its own character	rang gi mtshan nyid kyis yod pa	svalakṣaṇasat
eye consciousness	mig gi rnam shes	cakṣurvijñāna

familiarization	goms pa	abhyāsa
foe destroyer	dgra bcom pa	arhan/arhat
form body	gzugs sku	rūpakāya
fortune	sbyor ba	sampad
fruit	'bras bu	phala

giving	sbyin pa	dāna
god	lha	deva
great compassion	snying rje chen po	mahākaruṇā
Great Exposition School	bye brag smra ba	vaibhāṣika
Great Vehicle	theg chen	mahāyāna
ground	sa	bhūmi

hatred	zhe sdang	dveṣa
hearer	nyan thos	śrāvaka
hell being	dmyal ba	nāraka
highest yoga tantra	rnal 'byor bla med kyi rgyud	anuttarayogatantra
human	mi	manuṣya
hungry ghost	yi dvags	preta

ignorance	ma rig pa	avidyā
impermanence	mi rtag pa	anitya
imprint	lag rjes	
independent	rang dbang can	svatantra
inference	rjes dpag	anumāna

inherently established	rang bzhin gyis grub pa	svabhāvasiddha
inherently existent	rang bzhin gyis yod pa	*svabhāvasat
innate	lhan skyes	sahaja
innate afflictive emotion	nyon mongs lhan skyes	*sahajakleśa
intention to repay kindness	drin gzo ba	
interdependence	phan tshun rten pa	
intermediate state	bar do	antarābhāva

Jainism	rgyal ba pa	jaina
jealousy	phrag dog	īrṣyā
joy	dga' ba	muditā/prīti

latencies	bag chags/bag la nyal ba	vāsanā
leisure	dal ba	kṣaṇa
Lesser Vehicle	theg dman	hīnayāna
liberation	thar pa	mokṣa
love	byams pa	maitrī

Mīmāṃsaka	dpyod pa pa/ spyod pa pa	mīmāṃsaka
manifest	mngon gyur	abhimukhī
mantra	sngags	mantra
Mantra Vehicle	sngags kyi theg pa	mantrayāna
meditation	sgom pa	bhāvanā
meditative equipoise	mnyam bzhag	samāhita
meditative stabilization	ting nge 'dzin	samādhi
mental consciousness	yid kyi rnam shes	manovijñāna
mental continuum	sems rgyud	*cittasaṃtāna
merit	bsod nams	puṇya
method	thabs	upāya

Middle Way Autonomy School	dbu ma rang rgyud pa	svātantrikamādhyamika
Middle Way Consequence School	dbu ma thal 'gyur pa	prāsaṅgikamādhyamika
Middle Way School	dbu ma pa	mādhyamika
mind	sems	citta
mind of enlightenment	byang chub kyi sems	bodhicitta
mind only	sems tsam	cittamātra
Mind-Only School	sems tsam pa	cittamātra
miserliness	ser sna	mātsarya
mode of subsistence	gnas tshul/gnas lugs	
motivation	kun slong	

nature	ngo bo nyid	svabhāvatā
nirvāṇa	mya ngan las 'das pa	nirvāṇa
nirvāṇa with remainder	lhag bcas myang 'das	sopadhiśeṣanirvāṇa
nirvāṇa without remainder	lhag med myang 'das	nirupadhiśeṣanirvāṇa
nominal existent	btags pa tsam du yod pa	prajñāptisat
non-conceptual	rtog med	nirvikalpaka
non-duality of profound and manifest	zab gsal gnyis med	
nose consciousness	sna'i rnam shes	ghrāṇavijñāna

object of engagement	'jug yul	*pravṛttiviṣaya
objective view	yul gyi lta ba	
obstruction	sgrib pa	nivaraṇa
obstructions to liberation/ afflictive obstructions	nyon mongs pa'i sgrib pa	kleśāvaraṇa
obstructions to omniscience	shes bya'i sgrib pa	jñeyāvaraṇa
odor	dri	gandha
omniscience	rnam mkhyen	sarvākārajñāna

path	lam	mārga

path of accumulation	tshogs lam	saṃbhāramārga
path of meditation	sgom lam	bhāvanāmārga
path of no more learning	mi slob lam	aśaikṣamārga
path of preparation	sbyor lam	prayogamārga
path of seeing	mthong lam	darśanamārga
patience	bzod pa	kṣānti
Perfection Vehicle	phar phyin kyi theg pa	pāramitāyāna
perfections	phar phyin	pāramitā
performance tantra	spyod rgyud	caryātantra
person	gang zag/skyes bu	pudgala/puruṣa
phenomenon	chos	dharma
practical mind of enlightenment	'jug sems	
prayer petition	smon lam	praṇidhāna
predisposition	bag chags	vāsanā
pride	nga rgyal	māna
product	byas pa	kṛta
profound	zab mo	gambhīra
pure land	dag zhing	kṣetraśuddhi
quintessential instruction	man ngag	upadeśa
reality	chos nyid	dharmatā
realization	rtogs pa	
refuge	skyabs	śaraṇa
reification	sgro btags	samāropa
Sāṃkhya	grangs can	sāṃkhya
sūtra	mdo	sūtra
Sūtra School	mdo sde pa	sautrāntika
self	bdag	ātman
self-cherishing	rang gces 'dzin	
selfless	bdag med	nairātmya
self-sufficient	rang rkya thub pa	
sentient being	sems can	sattva

separate entity	ngo bo tha dad	
shape	dbyibs	saṃstāna
solitary realizer	rang sangs rgyas	pratyekabuddha
sound	sgra	śabda
space	nam mkha'	ākāśa
spacelike equipoise	nam mkha' lta bu'i mnyam bzhag	
special insight	lhag mthong	vipaśyanā
stability	gnas cha	
stabilizing meditation	'jog sgom	
subjective view	yul can gyi lta ba	
substantially existent	rdzas su yod pa	dravyasat
substantially existent person	rdzas yod kyi gang zag	dravyasatpudgala
subtle selflessness of people	gang zag gi bdag med phra mo	
suchness	de nyid/de kho na nyid	tathatā
suffering	sdug bsngal	duḥkha

---

tangible object	reg bya	spraṣṭavya
tantra	rgyud	tantra
taste	ro	rasa
teaching	bstan pa	śāsana
tenet system	grub mtha'	siddhānta
Three Jewels	dkon mchog gsum	triśaraṇa
tongue consciousness	lce'i rnam shes	jihvāvijñāna
trainee	gdul bya	vineya
transmigrator/ transmigrations	'gro ba	gati
true cessation	'gog bden	nirodhasatya
true path	lam bden	mārgasatya
truth body	chos sku	dharmakāya
two truths	bden pa gnyis	satyadvaya

ultimate mind of enlightenment	don dam byang chub kyi sems	paramārthabodhicitta
ultimate truth	don dam bden pa	paramārthasatya
union	zung 'brel/zung 'jug	yuganaddha
unitary	gcig	ekatva

Vajra Vehicle	rdo rje theg pa	vajrayāna
Vajrasattva	rdo rje sems dpa'	vajrasattva
vehicle	theg pa	yāna
visible form	gzugs	rūpa

wind	rlung	prāṇa
wisdom	shes rab	prajñā

yoga tantra	rnal 'byor rgyud	yogatantra
Yogic Autonomy Middle Way School	rnal 'byor spyod pa'i dbu ma rang rgyud pa	yogācārasvātantrika-mādhyamika

NOTES

---

[1] Wilfred Cantwell Smith, "Comparative Religion: Whither—and Why?" in *The History of Religions, Essays in Methodology*, ed. Mircea Eliade and Joseph M. Kitagawa (Chicago: The University of Chicago Press, 1959), pp. 31–66, and especially p. 34.

[2] For a brief discussion of the ills of cultural determinism, see Joachim Wach, *The Comparative Study of Religions*, ed. Joseph M. Kitagawa (New York: Columbia University Press, 1958), p. 57.

[3] The first series was given in 1974 in conjunction with Khetsun Sangpo Rinbochay's lectures that were published as *Tantric Practice in Nyingma* (London: Rider, 1982; reprint, Ithaca, N.Y.: Snow Lion, 1982). The second series was given in 1978 on the difference between sūtra and tantra after the completion of a volume on that topic: H.H. the Dalai Lama, Tsong-ka-pa, and Jeffrey Hopkins, *Tantra in Tibet* (London: George Allen and Unwin, 1977; reprint, Ithaca, N.Y.: Snow Lion, 1987).

[4] *dbu ma thal 'gyur pa, prāsaṅgikamādhyamika.*

[5] *tsong kha pa blo bzang grags pa;* 1357–1419.

[6] *dge lugs pa.*

[7] See Jeffrey Hopkins, *Emptiness in the Mind-Only School of Buddhism* (Berkeley: University of California Press, 1999), p. 68.

[8] Paraphrasing *gung thang dkon mchog bstan pa'i sgron me* (1762–1823); *Beginnings of a Commentary on the Difficult Points of [Ḏzong-ka-ḇa's] "Differentiating the Interpretable and the Definitive": Quintessence of "The*

Essence of Eloquence" (drang nges rnam 'byed kyi dka' 'grel rtsom 'phro legs bshad snying po'i yang snying) (Sarnath, India: Guru Deva, 1965), p. 17.7–17.16. For a brief biography, see E. Gene Smith, *University of Washington Tibetan Catalogue* (Seattle: University of Washington Press, 1969), 1: 81–82.

⁹ For his life story, see Lobsang Gyatso, *Memoirs of a Tibetan Lama*, translated and edited by Gareth Sparham (Ithaca, N.Y.: Snow Lion, 1998).

¹⁰ With respect to the translation of *arhan/arhant (dgra bcom pa)* as "foe destroyer," I do this to accord with the usual Tibetan translation of the term and to assist in capturing the flavor of oral and written traditions that frequently refer to this etymology. Arhants or "foe destroyers" *(arihan)* have overcome *(han* means to kill) the foe *(ari* means enemy) that is the afflictive emotions *(nyon mongs, kleśa)*, the chief of which is ignorance.

The Indian and Tibetan translators of Sanskrit and other texts into Tibetan were also aware of the etymology of *arhant* as "worthy one," as they translated the name of the "founder" of the Jaina system, Arhat, as *mchod 'os* ("Worthy of Worship"). (See Jam-ȳang-shay-b̄a, *Great Exposition of Tenets, ka* 62a.3.)

They were also aware of Chandrakīrti's gloss of the term as "worthy one" in his *Clear Words: sadevamānuṣāsurāl lokāt pūnārhatvād arhannityuchyate* (Louis de la Vallée Poussin, *Mūlamadhyamakakārikās de Nāgārjuna avec la Prasannapadā Commentaire de Candrakīrti*, Bibliotheca Buddhica 4 [Osnabrück, Germany: Biblio Verlag, 1970], 486.5); *lha dang mi dang lha ma yin du bcas pa'i 'jig rten gyis mchod par 'os pas dgra bcom pa zhes brjod la* (Tibetan Cultural Printing Press edition, 409.20; also, P. 5260, vol. 98, 75.2.2): "Because of being worthy of worship by the world of gods, humans, and demigods, they are called arhants."

Also, they were aware of Haribhadra's twofold etymology in his *Illumination of the Eight Thousand Stanza Perfection of Wisdom Sūtra.* In reference to the epithets of the Buddha's retinue, Haribhadra says: "They are called *arhant* [Worthy Ones, from the root *arh* "to be worthy"] since they are worthy of worship, religious donations, and being assembled together in a group, and so forth." (Unrai Wogihara,

Abhisamayālaṃkārālokā Prajñā-pāramitā-vyākhyā [Tokyo: Toyo Bunko, 1932–1935; reprint, Tokyo: Sankibo Buddhist Book Store, 1973], 9.8–9: *sarva evātra pūjā-dakṣiṇā-gaṇa-parikarṣādy-ārhatayarhantaḥ;* P. 5189, vol. 90, 67.5.7: *'dir thams cad kyang mchod pa dang // yon dang tshogs su 'dub la sogs par 'os pas na dgra bcom pa'o.*)

Also: "They are called *arhant* [foe destroyer, *arihan*] because they have destroyed *[hata]* the foe *[ari]*." (Wogihara, *Abhisamayālaṃkārālokā,* 10.18: *hatāritvād arhantaḥ;* P. 5189, vol. 90, 69.3.6: *dgra rnams bcom pas na dgra bcom pa'o.*) (My thanks to Dr. Gareth Sparham for the references to Haribhadra.)

Thus, we are dealing with a considered preference in the face of alternative etymologies. Unfortunately, there is no one word in English that can convey both this meaning and "worthy of worship," so I have gone with what clearly has become the predominant meaning in Tibet.

For an excellent discussion of the two etymologies of arhat in Buddhism and Jainism, see L. M. Joshi, *Facets of Jaina Religiousness in Comparative Light,* L. D. Series 85 (Ahmedabad, India: L.D. Institute of Indology, 1981), pp. 53–58.

[11] See Jeffrey Hopkins, *Buddhist Advice for Living and Liberation: Nāgārjuna's Precious Garland* (Ithaca, N.Y.: Snow Lion, 1998), p. 66, p. 140.

[12] Eye, ear, nose, tongue, and body sense consciousnesses.

[13] Visual forms (that is, colors and shapes), sounds, odors, tastes, and tangible objects.

[14] See Jeffrey Hopkins, *Buddhist Advice for Living and Liberation,* p. 43, p. 144.

[15] Dzong-ka-ba cites this stanza in his *The Essence of Eloquence (legs bshad snying po);* see Jeffrey Hopkins, *Emptiness in the Mind-Only School of Buddhism,* p. 71.

[16] See Lati Rinbochay and Jeffrey Hopkins, *Death, Intermediate State and Rebirth in Tibetan Buddhism* (London: Rider, 1979; Ithaca, N.Y.: Snow Lion, 1981).

[17] The term "Lesser Vehicle" (theg dman, hīnayāna) has its origin in the writings of Great Vehicle (theg chen, mahāyāna) authors and was, of course, not used by those to whom it was ascribed. Substitutes such as "non-Mahāyāna," "Nikāya Buddhism," and "Theravādayāna" have been suggested in order to avoid the pejorative sense of "Lesser." However, "Lesser Vehicle" is a convenient term in this particular context for a type of tenet system or practice that is seen in Tibetan scholarship to be surpassed, but not negated by, a "higher" system. The Lesser Vehicle is not despised, most of it being incorporated into the Great Vehicle. The monks' and nuns' vows are Lesser Vehicle, as is much of the course of study in Ge-luk-ba monastic universities—years of study are put into the topics of epistemology *(tshad ma, pramāṇa)*, manifest knowledge *(chos mngon pa, abhidharma)*, and discipline *('dul ba, vinaya)*, all of which are mostly Lesser Vehicle in perspective.

[18] The world "altruism" is built from the Latin "alter," which means "other"; thus the word means "otherism" and has no connection with the word "true."

[19] The term "maṇḍala" is most often used to refer to a divine environment—a palace and its surroundings—as well as the deities that reside there; thus there are residence maṇḍalas and resident maṇḍalas. However, here the term "maṇḍala" refers to the world system in glorified aspect; see H.H. the Dalai Lama and Jeffrey Hopkins, *The Kālachakra Tantra: Rite of Initiation* (London: Wisdom, 1985; 2d rev. ed. 1989), p. 75.

[20] The discussion here will be according to Dzong-ka-ba's presentation.

[21] The so-called Lesser Vehicle schools teach only a selflessness of persons, whereas the Great Vehicle schools teach a selflessness of all phenomena.

[22] *bye brag smra ba, vaibhāṣika.*

[23] *mdo sde pa, sautrāntika.*

[24] *sems tsam pa, cittamātra.*

[25] *dbu ma pa, mādhyamika.*

[26] *rang rgyud pa, svātantrika.*

[27] *thal 'gyur pa, prāsaṅgika.*

[28] See T.R.V. Murti, *The Central Philosophy of Buddhism* (London: George Allen and Unwin, 1960), p. 247.

[29] Tenzin Gyatso, *The Buddhism of Tibet* (London: George Allen and Unwin, 1983; reprint, Ithaca, N.Y.: Snow Lion, 1987), p. 56.

[30] See Geshe Lhundup Sopa and Jeffrey Hopkins, *Cutting through Appearances: The Practice and Theory of Tibetan Buddhism* (Ithaca, N.Y.: Snow Lion, 1989), pp. 166–67.

[31] The Yogic Autonomy Middle Way School holds that solitary realizers realize the coarse selflessness of phenomena; see Geshe Lhundup Sopa and Jeffrey Hopkins, *Cutting through Appearances*, p. 290.

[32] These are taken from Jeffrey Hopkins' Supplement in H.H. the Dalai Lama, Tsong-ka-pa, and Jeffrey Hopkins, *Tantra in Tibet*, pp. 210–14.

[33] See Tenzin Gyatso, *The Buddhism of Tibet*, p. 56.

[34] Great Vehicle foe destroyers are buddhas.

[35] See Dzong-ka-ba's extensive presentation of this point in Kensur Lekden, Tsong-kha-pa, and Jeffrey Hopkins, *Compassion in Tibetan Buddhism* (London: Rider, 1980; reprint, Ithaca, N.Y.: Snow Lion, 1980), pp. 150–81.

[36] Of course, these facts do not make it the best.

[37] Quoted from the exposition of special insight by the Fifth Dalai Lama Nga-wang-lo-sang-gya-tso (*ngag dbang blo bzang rgya mtsho,* 1617–1682) in his *Instruction on the Stages of the Path to Enlightenment, Sacred Word of Mañjushrī (byang chub lam gyi rim pa'i khrid yig 'jam pa'i dbyangs kyi zhal lung)* (Thimphu: Kun-bzang-stobs-rgyal, 1976) as found in Jeffrey Hopkins, trans., *Practice of Emptiness* (Dharamsala: Library of Tibetan Works and Archives, 1974), p. 21.

[38] Emptiness is called a truth because it exists the way it appears in direct perception.

[39] See Jeffrey Hopkins, *Meditation on Emptiness* (London: Wisdom, 1983; rev. ed. Boston: Wisdom, 1996), pp. 863–64, n. 521.

[40] Subsistence here means being or abiding; it does not mean "barely getting by" as in subsistence farming.

[41] See the Dalai Lama's introduction in H.H. the Dalai Lama, Tsong-ka-pa, and Jeffrey Hopkins, *The Yoga of Tibet* (London: George Allen and Unwin), 1981; reprinted as *Deity Yoga* (Ithaca, N.Y.: Snow Lion, 1987), pp. 33–35.

[42] See the Dalai Lama's introduction in H.H. the Dalai Lama, Tsong-ka-pa, and Jeffrey Hopkins, *Tantra in Tibet*, p. 70.

[43] See the Dalai Lama's introduction in H.H. the Dalai Lama, Tsong-ka-pa, and Jeffrey Hopkins, *Tantra in Tibet* , pp. 15–48 and p. 76.

[44] Geshe Lhundup Sopa reported this.

[45] Jam-yang-shay-ba, *Great Exposition of the Middle/Analysis of [Chandrakīrti's] "Supplement to [Nāgārjuna's] 'Treatise on the Middle'": Treasury of Scripture and Reasoning: Thoroughly Illuminating the Profound Meaning [of Emptiness], Entrance for the Fortunate (dbu ma chen mo/dbu ma jug pa'i mtha' dpyod lung rigs gter mdzod zab don kun gsal skal bzang 'jug ngogs)* (Buxaduar: Gomang, 1967), 48a.5–49a.1.

BIBLIOGRAPHY

Sūtras and tantras are listed alphabetically by English title in the first section of the bibliography. Indian and Tibetan treatises are listed alphabetically by author in the second section; other works are listed alphabetically by author in the third section.

"P.," standing for "Peking edition," refers to the *Tibetan Tripiṭaka* (Tokyo-Kyoto: Tibetan Tripiṭaka Research Foundation, 1956). Works mentioned in the first or second sections are sometimes not repeated in the third section.

1. Sūtras and Tantras
Kāshyapa Chapter Sūtra
kāśyapaparivartasūtra
'od srung gi le'u'i mdo
P. 760.43, vol. 24

Sanskrit: Alexander von Staël-Holstein. *Kāśyapaparivarta: A Mahāyanasūtra of the Ratnakūpa Class*. Shanghai: Commercial Press, 1926; reprint, Tokyo: Meicho-fukyū-kai, 1977.

English translation: Garma C. C. Chang, ed. *A Treasury of Mahāyāna Sūtras*. University Park: Pennsylvania State University Press, 1983.

2. Other Sanskrit and Tibetan Works
Chandrakīrti (*candrakīrti, zla ba grags pa,* seventh century)
  Clear Words, Commentary on (Nāgārjuna's) "Treatise on the Middle"
  mūlamadhyamakavṛttiprasannapadā
  dbu ma rtsa ba'i 'grel pa tshig gsal ba
  P. 5260, vol. 98. Also: Dharamsala, India: Tibetan Cultural Printing Press, 1968.

Sanskrit: Louis de la Vallée Poussin. *Mūlamadhyamakakārikās de Nāgārjuna avec la Prasannapadā commentaire de Candrakīrti.* Bibliotheca Buddhica 4. Osnabrück, Germany: Biblio Verlag, 1970.

English translation (chap. 1, 25): T. Stcherbatsky. *Conception of Buddhist Nirvāṇa,* 77–222. Leningrad: Office of the Academy of Sciences of the USSR, 1927; rev. ed., Delhi: Motilal Banarsidass, 1978.

English translation (chap. 2): Jeffrey Hopkins. *Chandrakirti's Analysis of Coming and Going.* Dharamsala, India: Library of Tibetan Works and Archives, 1974.

Partial English translation: Mervyn Sprung. *Lucid Exposition of the Middle Way: The Essential Chapters from the Prasannapadā of Candrakīrti translated from the Sanskrit.* London: Routledge, 1979; Boulder, Co.: Prajna Press, 1979.

French translation (chaps. 2–4, 6–9, 11, 23, 24, 26, 28): Jacques May. *Prasannapadā Madhyamaka-vṛtti, douze chapitres traduits du sanscrit et du tibétain.* Paris: Adrien-Maisonneuve, 1959.

French translation (chaps. 18–22): J. W. de Jong. *Cinq chapitres de la Prasannapadā.* Paris: Geuthner, 1949.

French translation (chap. 17): É. Lamotte. "Le Traité de l'acte de Vasubandhu, Karmasiddhiprakaraṇa," *Mélanges Chinois et Bouddhiques* 4 (1936): 265–88.

German translation (chap. 5, 12–26): Stanislaw Schayer. *Ausgewählte Kapitel aus der Prasannapadā.* Krakow: Polskiej Akademji Umiejetnosci, 1931.

German translation (chap. 10): Stanislaw Schayer. "Feuer und Brennstoff." *Rocznik Orjentalistyczny* 7 (1931): 26–52.

Dzong-ka-ba Lo-sang-drak-ba (*tsong kha pa blo bzang grags pa,* 1357–1419)

    Great Exposition of Secret Mantra/The Stages of the Path to a Conqueror and Pervasive Master, a Great Vajradhara: Revealing All Secret Topics
    sngags rim chen mo/rgyal ba khyab bdag rdo rje 'chang chen po'i lam gyi rim pa gsang ba kun gyi gnad rnam par phye ba

P. 6210, vol. 161. Also: Delhi: Ngawang Gelek, 1975. Also: Delhi: Guru Deva, 1979.

English translation (chap. 1): H.H. the Dalai Lama, Tsong-ka-pa, and Jeffrey Hopkins. *Tantra in Tibet*. London: George Allen and Unwin, 1977; reprint, Ithaca, N.Y.: Snow Lion, 1987.

English translation (chap. 2–3): H.H. the Dalai Lama, Tsong-ka-pa, and Jeffrey Hopkins. *The Yoga of Tibet*. London: George Allen and Unwin, 1981; reprinted as *Deity Yoga*. Ithaca, N.Y.: Snow Lion, 1987.

Treatise Differentiating the Interpretable and the Definitive: The Essence of Eloquence
drang ba dang nges pa'i don rnam par phye ba'i bstan bcos legs bshad snying po
Collected Works of Rje Tsoṅ-kha-pa Blo-bzaṅ-grags-pa. Vol. 21 pha, 478–714. Delhi: Ngawang Gelek Demo, 1975. For other editions see the translation by Jeffrey Hopkins, listed just below, p. 355.

English translation (prologue and Mind-Only section): Jeffrey Hopkins. *Emptiness in the Mind-Only School of Buddhism*. Berkeley: University of California Press, 1999.

English translation: Robert A.F. Thurman. *Tsong Khapa's Speech of Gold in the Essence of True Eloquence*. Princeton, N.J.: Princeton University Press, 1984, pp. 185–385.

Chinese translation: Venerable Fa Zun. "Bian Liao Yi Bu Liao Yi Shuo Cang Lun." In *Xi Zang Fo Jiao Jiao Yi Lun Ji*. Vol. 2, pp. 159–276. Taipei: Da Sheng Wen Hua Chu Ban She, 1979.

Gung-tang Ḡön-chok-d̄en-b̄ay-drön-may (*gung thang dkon mchog bstan pa'i sgron me, 1762–1823*)
Beginnings of a Commentary on the Difficult Points of [D̄zong-ka-b̄a's] "Differentiating the Interpretable and the Definitive": Quintessence of "The Essence of Eloquence"
drang nges rnam 'byed kyi dka' 'grel rtsom 'phro legs bshad snying po'i yang snying

Collected Works of Guṅ-thaṅ Dkon-mchog-bstan-pa'i-sgron-me. Vol. I, pp. 403–723. New Delhi: Ngawang Gelek Demo, 1975. Also: Sarnath, India: Guru Deva, 1965.

Jam-ȳang-shay-b̄a Nga-w̄ang-d̄zön-drü (*'jam dbyangs bzhad pa ngag dbang brtson grus*, 1648–1722)

Great Exposition of Tenets/Explanation of "Tenets": Sun of the Land of Samantabhadra Brilliantly Illuminating All of Our Own and Others' Tenets and the Meaning of the Profound [Emptiness], Ocean of Scripture and Reasoning Fulfilling All Hopes of All Beings

grub mtha' chen mo/grub mtha'i rnam bshad rang gzhan grub mtha' kun dang zab don mchog tu gsal ba kun bzang zhing gi nyi ma lung rigs rgya mtsho skye dgu'i re ba kun skong

Edition cited: Musoorie, India: Dalama, 1962. Also: *Collected Works of 'Jam-dbyaṅs-bzad-pa'i-rdo-rdo-rje*. Vol. 14. New Delhi: Ngawang Gelek Demo, 1973.

English translation (beginning of the chapter on the Consequence School): Jeffrey Hopkins. *Meditation on Emptiness*. London: Wisdom, 1983; rev. ed. Boston: Wisdom, 1996. Pp. 581–697.

Great Exposition of the Middle/Analysis of [Chandrakīrti's] "Supplement to [Nāgārjuna's] 'Treatise on the Middle'": Treasury of Scripture and Reasoning, Thoroughly Illuminating the Profound Meaning [of Emptiness], Entrance for the Fortunate

dbu ma chen mo/dbu ma 'jug pa'i mtha' dpyod lung rigs gter mdzod zab don kun gsal skal bzang 'jug ngogs

Edition cited: Buxaduar, India: Go-mang, 1967. Also: *Collected Works of 'Jam-dbyaṅs-bzad-pa'i-rdo-rdo-rje*. Vol. 9. New Delhi: Ngawang Gelek Demo, 1973.

Nāgārjuna (*klu sgrub*, first to second century, C.E.)

Precious Garland of Advice for the King
rājaparikathāratnāvalī
rgyal po la gtam bya ba rin po che'i phreng ba
P. 5658, vol. 129

Sanskrit, Tibetan, and Chinese: Michael Hahn. *Nāgārjuna's*

Ratnāvalī. Vol. 1. *The Basic Texts (Sanskrit, Tibetan, and Chinese)*. Bonn: Indica et Tibetica Verlag, 1982.

English translation: Jeffrey Hopkins. *Buddhist Advice for Living and Liberation: Nāgārjuna's Precious Garland*. Pp. 94–164. Ithaca, New York: Snow Lion, 1998. Supercedes that in: Nāgārjuna and the Seventh Dalai Lama. *The Precious Garland and the Song of the Four Mindfulnesses*. Translated and edited by Jeffrey Hopkins and Lati Rinbochay, with Anne Klein. Pp. 17–93. London: George Allen and Unwin, 1975; New York: Harper and Row, 1975; reprint in H.H. the Dalai Lama, Tenzin Gyatso. *The Buddhism of Tibet*. London: George Allen and Unwin, 1983; reprint, Ithaca, New York: Snow Lion, 1987.

English translation: John Dunne and Sara McClintock. *The Precious Garland: An Epistle to a King*. Boston: Wisdom, 1997.

English translation of 223 stanzas (chap. 1, 1–77; chap. 2, 1–46; chap 4; 1–100): Giuseppe Tucci. "The *Ratnāvalī* of Nāgārjuna." *Journal of the Royal Asiatic Society* (1934): 307–25; (1936): 237–52, 423–35.

Japanese translation: Uryūzu, Ryushin. *Butten II, Sekai Koten Bungaku Zenshū* 7 (July, 1965): 349–72. Edited by Nakamura, Hajime. Tokyo: Chikuma Shobo. Also: Uryūzu, Ryushin. *Daijo Butten* 14 (1974): 231–316. *Ryūju Ronshū*. Edited by Kajiyama, Yuichi, and Uryūzu, Ryushin. Tokyo: Chūokoronsha.

Danish translation: Christian Lindtner. *Nagarjuna, Juvelkaeden og andre skrifter*. Copenhagen: 1980.

Treatise on the Middle/Fundamental Treatise on the Middle, Called "Wisdom"
madhyamakaśāstra/prajñānāmamūlamadhyamakakārika
dbu ma'i bstan bcos/dbu ma rtsa ba'i tshig le'ur byas pa shes rab ces bya ba
P. 5224, vol. 95

Sanskrit: J. W. de Jong. *Nāgārjuna, Mūlamadhya-makakārikāḥ*. Madras, India: Adyar Library and Research Centre, 1977; reprint,

Wheaton, Ill.: Agents, Theosophical Publishing House, c. 1977. Also: Christian Lindtner. *Nāgārjuna's Filosofiske Vaerker,* 177–215. Indiske Studier 2. Copenhagen: Akademisk Forlag, 1982.

English translation: Frederick Streng. *Emptiness: A Study in Religious Meaning.* Nashville, Tenn.: Abingdon Press, 1967. Also: Kenneth Inada. *Nāgārjuna: A Translation of His Mūlamadhyamakakārikā.* Tokyo: Hokuseido Press, 1970. Also: David J. Kalupahana. *Nāgārjuna: The Philosophy of the Middle Way.* Albany, N.Y.: State University Press of New York, 1986. Also: Jay L. Garfield. *The Fundamental Wisdom of the Middle Way.* New York: Oxford University Press, 1995.

Italian translation: R. Gnoli. *Nāgārjuna: Madhyamaka Kārikā, Le stanze del cammino di mezzo.* Enciclopedia di autori classici 61. Turin, Italy: P. Boringhieri, 1961.

Danish translation: Christian Lindtner. *Nāgārjuna's Filosofiske Vaerker.* Pp. 67–135. Indiske Studier 2. Copenhagen: Akademisk Forlag, 1982.

Nga-w̄ang-l̄o-sang-gya-tso (*ngag dbang blo bzang rgya mtsho,* Fifth Dalai Lama, 1617–1682)
Instructions on the Stages of the Path to Enlightenment: Sacred Word of Mañjushrī
byang chub lam gyi rim pa'i 'khrid yig 'jam pa'i dbyangs kyi zhal lung
Thimphu, Bhutan: Kun bzang stobs rgyal, 1976.

English translation of the "Perfection of Wisdom" chapter: Jeffrey Hopkins. *Practice of Emptiness.* Dharamsala: Library of Tibetan Works and Archives, 1974.

Shāntideva (*zhi ba lha,* eighth century)
Engaging in the Bodhisattva Deeds
bodhi[sattva]caryāvatāra
byang chub sems dpa'i spyod pa la 'jug pa
P. 5272, vol. 99

Sanskrit: P. L. Vaidya. *Bodhicaryāvatāra.* Buddhist Sanskrit Texts, 12. Darbhanga, India: Mithila Institute, 1988.

Sanskrit and Tibetan: Vidhushekara Bhattacharya. *Bodhicaryāvatāra*. Bibliotheca Indica, 280. Calcutta: The Asiatic Society, 1960.

Sanskrit and Tibetan with Hindi translation: Rāmaśaṁkara Tripāṭhī, ed. *Bodhicaryāvatāra*. Bauddha-Himālaya-Granthamālā, 8. Leh, Ladākh: Central Institute of Buddhist Studies, 1989.

English translation: Stephen Batchelor. *A Guide to the Bodhisattva's Way of Life*. Dharamsala, India: Library of Tibetan Works and Archives, 1979. Also: Marion Matics. *Entering the Path of Enlightenment*. New York: Macmillan, 1970. Also: Kate Crosby and Andrew Skilton. *The Bodhicaryāvatāra*. Oxford: Oxford University Press, 1996. Also: Padmakara Translation Group. *The Way of the Bodhisattva*. Boston: Shambhala, 1997. Also: Vesna A. Wallace and B. Alan Wallace. *A Guide to the Bodhisattva Way of Life*. Ithaca, N.Y.: Snow Lion, 1997.

Contemporary commentary by H.H. the Dalai Lama, Tenzin Gyatso. *Transcendent Wisdom*. Ithaca, N.Y.: Snow Lion, 1988. Also: H.H. the Dalai Lama, Tenzin Gyatso. *A Flash of Lightning in the Dark of the Night*. Boston: Shambhala, 1994.

3. Other Works

Gyatso, Lobsang. *Memoirs of a Tibetan Lama*. Translated and edited by Gareth Sparham. Ithaca, N.Y.: Snow Lion, 1998.

H.H. the Dalai Lama, Tenzin Gyatso. *Buddhism of Tibet and the Key to the Middle Way*. Translated by Jeffrey Hopkins. London: George Allen and Unwin, 1975. Reprinted in a combined volume, *The Buddhism of Tibet*. London: George Allen and Unwin, 1983; reprint, Ithaca, N.Y.: Snow Lion, 1987.

H.H. the Dalai Lama, Tenzin Gyatso and Jeffrey Hopkins. *The Kālachakra Tantra: Rite of Initiation*. Translated and introduced by Jeffrey Hopkins. London: Wisdom, 1985; 2d rev. ed. 1989.

Hopkins, Jeffrey. *Emptiness Yoga: The Middle Way Consequence School*. Ithaca, N.Y.: Snow Lion, 1983.

————. *Meditation on Emptiness*. London: Wisdom, 1983; rev. ed. Boston: Wisdom, 1996.

Lati Rinbochay and Jeffrey Hopkins. *Death, Intermediate State and Rebirth*. London: Rider, 1979; Ithaca, N.Y.: Snow Lion, 1981.

Lekden, Kensur, Tsong-kha-pa, and Jeffrey Hopkins. *Compassion in Tibetan Buddhism*. London: Rider, 1980; reprint, Ithaca, N.Y.: Snow Lion, 1980.

Murti, T.R.V. *The Central Philosophy of Buddhism*. London: George Allen & Unwin, 1960.

Sangpo, Khetsun. *Tantric Practice in Nyingma*. Translated by Jeffrey Hopkins London: Rider, 1982; reprint, Ithaca, N.Y.: Snow Lion, 1982.

Smith, E. Gene. *University of Washington Tibetan Catalogue*. 2 vols. Seattle: University of Washington Press, 1969.

Smith, Wilfred Cantwell. "Comparative Religion: Whither—and Why?" In *The History of Religions, Essays in Methodology*. Edited by Mircea Eliade and Joseph M. Kitagawa. Chicago: The University of Chicago Press, 1959.

Sopa, Geshe Lhundup and Jeffrey Hopkins. *Practice and Theory of Tibetan Buddhism*. New York: Grove, 1976; rev. ed., *Cutting through Appearances: Practice and Theory of Tibetan Buddhism*. Ithaca, New York: Snow Lion, 1989.

Wach, Joachim. *The Comparative Study of Religions*. Edited by Joseph M. Kitagawa. New York: Columbia University Press, 1958.

Wogihara, Unrai. *Abhisamayālaṃkārālokā Prajñā-pāramitā-vyākhyā, The Work of Haribhadra*. 7 vols. Tokyo: Toyo Bunko, 1932–1935; reprint, Tokyo: Sankibo Buddhist Book Store, 1973.

Wylie, Turrell. "A Standard System of Tibetan Transcription." *Harvard Journal of Asiatic Studies* 22 (1959): 261–67.

INDEX

vows 97, 133, 156

wisdom
union of method and 59, 61,
133, 139
See also emptiness, direct realization of

yoga 58, 123, 134
See also deity yoga
yogis 45, 58, 126

ABOUT WISDOM PUBLICATIONS

Wisdom Publications, a not-for-profit publisher, is dedicated to making available authentic Buddhist works for the benefit of all. We publish translations of the sutras and tantras, commentaries and teachings of past and contemporary Buddhist masters, and original works by the world's leading Buddhist scholars. We publish our titles with the appreciation of Buddhism as a living philosophy and with the special commitment to preserve and transmit important works from all the major Buddhist traditions.

If you would like more information or a copy of our mail-order catalogue, please contact us at:

Wisdom Publications
199 Elm Street, Somerville, Massachusetts 02144, USA
Telephone: (617) 776-7416 • Fax: (617) 776-7841
E-mail: info@wisdompubs.org • http://www.wisdompubs.org

The Wisdom Trust

As a not-for-profit publisher, Wisdom Publications is dedicated to the publication of fine Dharma books for the benefit of all sentient beings and dependent upon the kindness and generosity of sponsors in order to do so. If you would like to make a donation to Wisdom, please do so through our Somerville office. If you would like to sponsor the publication of a book, please write or e-mail us for more information.

Thank you.

Wisdom Publications is a non-profit, charitable 501(c)(3) organization and a part of the Foundation for the Preservation of the Mahayana Tradition (FPMT).